Autistic Thinking –
This Is the Title

Peter Vermeulen

Foreword by Francesca Happé

Jessica Kingsley Publishers
London and Philadelphia

First published in the United Kingdom in 2001 by
Jessica Kingsley Publishers Ltd,
116 Pentonville Road,
London N1 9JB,
England
and
325 Chestnut Street,
Philadelphia, PA 19106, USA.

www.jkp.com

Library of Congress Cataloging in Publication Data
A CIP catalog record for this book is available from the Library of Congress

British Library Cataloguing in Publication Data
A CIP catalogue record for this book is available from the British Library

ISBN 1 85302 995 5

Printed and Bound in Great Britain by
Athenaeum Press, Gateshead, Tyne and Wear

'As a metaphor for Autism robots serve well in many respects.'
 – Uta Frith, *Autism: Explaining the Enigma* (1989, p. 46)

'*Aut ridenda omnia aut fledenda sunt.*'
('We must either laugh or cry about things.')
 – Seneca, *About Anger*, 2.10.

Contents

Special note

Throughout this book the word 'autism' is used as a synonym for 'autistic spectrum disorder'. Although there is some merit in arguing for the use of different labels within the autistic spectrum (e.g. Asperger syndrome), in terms of the understanding of the basic problem of all people with an autistic spectrum disorder – as described in this book – and in terms of treatment, a broad definition, encompassing the different disorders within the spectrum, is most appropriate.

Foreword

When you are in a foreign place, it helps to have a guide. Peter Vermeulen describes this book as a 'travelogue'. It is a nice metaphor: people with autism spectrum disorders often describe their experience of life as like being on an alien planet – Temple Grandin describes herself as like 'an anthropologist on Mars', and there is a website wonderfully titled 'Woops, wrong planet syndrome'! But in this book, the tables are turned, and we, the 'neurotypicals', travel for a little while in the land of logical, autistic thinking. This is a wonderful journey, in which we are helped by our guide's sense of humour and genuine respect for and understanding of people on the autism spectrum.

In the last few years, more and more people with autism spectrum disorders have come forward to share their experiences and insights, and to give a voice to autistic thinking. This exciting development has made clear the challenge for those living and working with autism. It is a challenge of mutual understanding, and a process of translation. Neurotypicals often talk about the difficulty people with autism have in understanding the intricacies and nuances of the social world, and the mistakes that are made. But it is clear that the failure of understanding can go both ways. We have no idea what it is to see the world through the eyes of autism. A highly intelligent and insightful young man with Asperger syndrome said, 'I wish the neurotypicals could be autistic for just one day – to see how it feels from the inside'. We offend the logic of the autistic mind, we confuse with indirect and non-literal language, we exasperate with our unpredictability and our social obsessions. Translation is vital, and Peter Vermeulen makes a great contribution towards that increased understanding with this small book. Anyone who reads it, and reads between the lines of the many wonderful anecdotes and examples, must surely be left with a greater respect of the autistic view of the world, and a sense of the value (as well as the challenge) of these very special minds.

Francesca Happé
Senior Scientist in Cognitive Psychology
Institute of Psychiatry, Kings College, London

'Just Describe Me as a Computer'
About this book

Computers and autism have something in common.

It is more than just a coincidence that intelligent individuals with autism express a special interest in computers. Many of them communicate with one another via the Internet, the worldwide network. And computers seem to function as excellent teaching tools for children with autism.

As early as 1943, Leo Kanner, the pioneer in describing autism, noticed the robotic link in children he was examining. Their behaviour somehow struck him as mechanical. It demonstrated an all too restrictive human sensitivity and it struck him as excessively rigid.[1] At that time, computers still belonged to the world of science fiction for most people. Today, at the turn of the 21st century, computers are part of our daily existence, with everybody becoming more and more familiar with the workings of these 'intelligent' machines. More and more people know how to push the right buttons and even children are talking about 'downloading', 'formatting', and 'surfing', as if it were just a matter of buttering toast for breakfast. Computers have ceased to be the magical, almighty and futuristic machines and have turned into everyday ordinary appliances.

Some of us in fact know more about computers than about the working of our microwave oven.

Some parents of autistic children who have experience in data processing, describe the behaviour and thinking of their children in computer terms. I have often heard the comment: 'If we don't program him, there is no output.' Or: 'If you don't push the right button, there is no reaction.' The manner in which computers process information is remarkably similar to the way in which individuals with autism process 'thought'.

The subject of this book is 'autistic thinking'. Not only have we acquired greater knowledge about the way computers perform, but we have also made tremendous strides forward in our scientific understanding of how individuals with autism think.

From the very beginning, autism has been recognised as a puzzling and strange disorder. It is surely no coincidence that many autistic societies take a piece of a jigsaw puzzle as their logo. Since the time of Leo Kanner, already over 50 years ago, parents, social assistants and researchers have been investigating the phenomenon. And while the puzzle is far from being solved, a number of pieces are falling into place, especially since well-known researchers have succeeded in understanding more about the 'strange' thought processes exhibited by individuals with autism. We haven't arrived there yet, but to get a clear idea of how individuals with autism think is the main key to solving the puzzle – even though we may never be able to put all the pieces together.

During the past 50 years, special attention has been paid to the *behaviour* of individuals with autism. The criteria for autism in the standard classification handbooks still refer to behaviour. No exclusive biological indicator has been found for autism. Medical doctors still cannot pinpoint the disturbance to one particular spot on the genome, as they can for instance for Down syndrome, where a count of chromosomes will give answers. And it does not appear as if autism can be linked to one specific location in the brain: there may be many causes. As long as we remain unable to fix autism in strict medical terms, we have to fall back on what is called 'behavioural diagnosis'. We observe the behaviour of an individual and draw up a diagnosis on the basis of these observations.

Behavioural diagnosis recognises different limiting factors. One of them pertains to the fact that many of the 'autistic behavioural patterns' are also exhibited in persons who don't have autism. Stereotyped behaviour also occurs in individuals with a learning disability. It is therefore incorrect to assume that anyone who displays stereotyped behaviour has autism. Furthermore, certain 'autistic characteristics' can be isolated in ordinary development.[2] Echolalia is a textbook example. 'Echolalia' refers to the act of repeating what you hear, in parrot fashion. A mother asks her child if he wants a cookie. 'Do you want a cookie?' The child answers: 'Do you want a cookie?' Echolalia is a normal phenomenon in language development. Many toddlers pass through this echolalistic stage.

The consideration of behaviour only will lead to a second limitation. Clearly, people with autism also are evolving: they learn new things, they absorb new experiences. This changes their behaviour. You need to have a good understanding of 'autistic behaviour' in general in order to keep track of the red thread running through 'autism'. As autistic behaviour is being 'watered down', it does not mean that the autism is disappearing. So the most pronounced limitation to the scrutiny of behaviour is this: autism can express itself in many different ways. A prototypical individual with autism simply does not exist. Autism is a disability of many aspects and the behaviour patterns of one person with autism are not entirely similar to the behaviour of another individual with autism. This means that some parents cannot quite recognise their children in accounts or stories that deal with autistic behaviour. The disorder is then simply labelled 'autism-related': this offers little comfort to parents in cases where it is the differences in a child's behaviour to the standard diagnosis which are particularly marked. The inflation of threshold diagnoses such as 'not otherwise specified' or 'related' is a product of the limitation of looking only at external behavioural manifestations.

There is a further problem with autism in that there is no common external characteristic as there is for other disorders such as Down syndrome. Individuals with Down syndrome generally have similar facial characteristics; they resemble one another. In contrast, similarities amongst people with autism, and what distinguishes individuals with autism from those without it, are interior characteristics: people with autism happen to think differently from people without autism. The essence of autism does not lie in external behaviour and is not outwardly visible. It is a problem of being unable to assign meaning to things. This is a problem shared by all persons with autism, yet the way in which this problem manifests itself (in behavioural terms) varies enormously.

Anybody wishing to gain a clearer understanding of autistic behaviour needs to get 'inside' the brain of a person with autism, or attempt to fit into his shoes, to find out how he – in complete contrast to ourselves – processes external auditory, visual, and physical experiences. Using this approach to gain knowledge about autistic thinking leads to a better understanding of people who have autism, and thus to an improved ability to help them.

Only quite recently, in the 1980s, did researchers seriously begin to study autistic thinking. This brought the level of knowledge in the field to a new phase. Scientific insights gained by these researchers have since been confirmed by first-hand reports. In the recent past, a number of individuals with autism have provided us with personal accounts of their disorder, their versions of the human experience. Their stories confirm the results of scientific studies.

We are striving to translate scientific insights into autistic thinking into concrete practice. This book places some tentative steps in that direction. I have attempted to assimilate recent scientific insight with the reports of individuals with autism. It is, of course, not possible to describe all aspects of autistic thinking and I have – as my feelings dictate – confined myself to treating the most essential of them all: the lack of coherent thinking.[3] Individuals with autism have difficulty interpreting the world as one integrated unit; they experience details as isolated units. In other words, they often fail to see the wood for the trees.

At present it is not quite clear how highly one should rate, in the total context of defining autism, the value of this discovery of a lack of coherent thought.[4] These new insights do not complete the puzzle but nonetheless allow a clearer picture of the whole. In this book I do not by any means offer an all-encompassing theory about autism. This is not at all the purpose. The book is not a scientific study, not a guideline with tables and statistics, although the concluding notes do refer to some academic literature on the subject.

This book is in many ways similar to a travelogue, a source that allows acquaintance with another world of thinking – a kind of collage about the often weird and wonderful convolutions that are so exclusive to the thinking process of individuals with autism. Just as in a travelogue, it is illustrated by anecdotes – experiences from auti-land.

The book is designed to give the reader a glimpse into the reality of autism: the very individual way in which those with autism process information. And it encompasses the entire spectrum of autistic disorders: from severe autism with additional learning disabilities to the related disorders, such as Asperger syndrome, and autism in combination with excellent skills. The whole of the auti-landscape: smooth and not-so-smooth.

And, in the final analysis, this book deviates also in one other aspect from the conventional texts about autism. Instead of the traditional theoretical expositions, case studies or summaries common in the relevant publications, I have opted for another way in which to present autism: the analogy. Two things are analogous to one another when they are not entirely identical but rather similar to each other. I have chosen two analogies: the computer and the jest.

'Just describe me as a computer, then I understand it better.' So said a young man with autism to his mentor, a professor of autism at the State University in Leiden. In this statement he indicates that computers can offer a comprehensible interpretation of this confusing disability. However, this anecdote was not the only motivation for choosing computers as models for autistic thinking. My own experience with computers constantly elicits the observation that it is not dissimilar to dealing with people with autism. To a colleague who is experiencing a problem with his computer I tend to remark, jokingly: 'Tackle your problem the way you would approach a person with autism. Be precise and clear in giving instructions. Everything will work out.'

But there is more. Having had many years of experience with artificial intelligence, I have found that the similarities between computer logic and autistic thinking are more concrete.[5] When reading a book about artificial intelligence, I get the feeling that I am reading about autism. Constantly I am confronted with things that make me remark: 'Wait a minute, I know that!' as in the following example: 'Computers have difficulty coping with the spirit of things: they prefer doing things by the book.'[6]

The same is said of people with autism. When Professor Ina van Berckelaer of Leiden University – the professor mentioned above – was offered the chair (professorship) 'Autism', she titled her address: 'Autism: To live by the book'.[7] The computer and living by the book provide two notions with an identical meaning: a literal interpretation. It is that notion of the 'literal interpretation' that computer logic and autistic thinking have in common with each other.

The second analogy is rather at variance with the first. It makes no comparison with mechanical thinking but instead something that is an essential part of human intelligence, something 'slippery': it is called 'humour'.[8] Computers are incapable of making up good jokes and they will never be able to do so. Likewise, individuals with autism have problems understanding the humorous talk and actions of other people around them. But, unwittingly, they themselves can be humorous in their own behaviour. Not only do many people with autism have a sense of humour (often of a very particular sort), but their qualitatively different behaviour can give rise to a smile too. Humorous anecdotes and jokes can contribute to explaining autism in ways other than those commonly used.

My choice for treating computers and jokes as analogues is not readily obvious. It is, in fact, controversial. I am fully aware of that.

The association of autism with computers could be interpreted as a low appreciation of autistic thinking in particular, and for individuals with autism in general. The worth of people, with or without autism, can hardly be compared with that of computers. I consider computers to be nothing else but (stupid) machines, while people with autism are human beings – people endowed with a heart and feelings, not with a Pentium processor. Because their thinking process is similar to that of a computer, people with autism are no less human than the rest of us who don't have autism. On the contrary, autistic thinking often demonstrates a special form of creativity and a sense of genius about which most people without autism can only fantasise. We are now learning that various famous artists of exceptional talent, such as Satie, Bartók, Bruckner and Kandinsky had autism.[9] Autism is not an inferior way of being; it is merely 'being different'. It is a challenge for every one of us to create a society wherein that kind of 'being different' will be allowed to occupy its legitimate position and exercise its legitimate rights as a component of our society.

To try to explain autism through jokes is, if possible, even more controversial. People with autism, and their families, have a tough time of it in our present society. Even specialists and professionals are often baffled to the extent that they do not know how to proceed with an individual with autism. One may well ask if it is appropriate to resort to levity in this sort of serious condition. For me, a humorous approach serves a double function.

Some famous person or other once said: 'What cannot be said in jest is not a serious matter.' Autism is – and I can confirm it – a serious disorder. But autism doesn't stop there and individuals with autism are more than the sum of their disorder. Individuals with autism are, first and foremost, 'different'. In their very own way they are primarily human and they have, like all other humans, their limitations and, also, their potential. Given the correct guidance, people with autism are capable of great achievements. Anyone who considers autism in an all-too-serious light, concentrating on the negatives and overlooking the positives, inevitably becomes very frustrated indeed. In order to avoid this sort of overly serious approach, it is perhaps worth trying a joke, now and then.

There is yet another way in which humor can put autism in a different light. Difficult and strange as the disability may be, both for the individual with autism herself and for those around her, autism is closer to us than we generally think. All of us have a touch of autism within us. The comparison with computers and jokes indicates that autism is not so outlandish as would appear at first sight. Autism shows us many of our own individual traits, but looked at through the magnifying glass. The jokes in this book are a bit like the mirrors at the old country fairs that showed us reflections of ourselves in exaggerated shapes. They show us the autism we carry around within ourselves, exaggerated of course, squashed together and all bunched up, or elongated and skinny.

The references to jokes and computers do in no way degrade autism, and are not meant to detract from the seriousness of the subject. What I have tried to do in using humour and analogy is to clarify autistic thinking so that the lay person may also get a clearer understanding of the disorder. The analogy with computers places autistic thinking in more concrete terms; the jokes humanise the whole. We need to either laugh or weep about things, wrote

Seneca, philosopher and minister of the notorious Roman Emperor Nero. Surely, we cannot only weep about autism…

Notes

1. Kanner (1943).

2. Susanne Leekam observed in her study (1996) that characteristics of autism were present in one-third of all neurologically typical young children. After five years of age, these autistic characteristics start to diminish.

3. 'Coherent thinking' is what Uta Frith (1989) calls *central coherence*. It refers to the ability for central coherence, for detecting cohesion in a combination of many stimuli.

4. For an overview of recent cognitive theories about autism and the merit of the 'central coherence' hypothesis, refer to Anthony Bailey *et al.* (1996).

5. I specifically found inspiration in the works of Douglas R. Hofstadter (1979 and especially 1985). The link between autism and computers or robots is in fact not new (see amongst others Frith 1989, pp.46–49).

6. Hofstadter (1985). (The quote is taken from the Dutch translation of 1988, p.552.)

7. van Berckelaer-Onnes (1992).

8. The inspiration for anecdotes in this book is less easy to state than the one related to computers. Jokes are in the public domain and I don't know who the authors are of many of them. I do know, however, that none is mine and that I have copied liberally. The anecdotes I have collected from my own experience and especially from parents. As 'experts in experience', parents are the main sources for illustrative materials.

9. Gillberg (1990) and Vermeulen (1998).

CHAPTER I

Unexpected Originality
About humour and autism

'People with an autistic spectrum disorder lack a sense of humour.'
I often hear and read this statement and it seems to be a common
belief. Even in the first publications on autism, one reads that
humour is far beyond the capabilities of an autistic mind. Hans
Asperger noted that people with autism 'never achieve that particular wisdom and deep intuitive human understanding that
underlie genuine humour'.[1]

Indeed, people with autism often find themselves baffled and
astonished by the humour of people without autism. This is often a
consequence of the problems with communication that are
involved in autism. A sense of humour depends on the ability to
understand the complex game of language, especially the ability to
'read between the lines'. In humour a lot is left unsaid.[2] If you listen
only to what is being said, then most jokes do not make sense. A
second explanation for the difficulties with humour that people
with autism have lies in their problems with the social aspects of
communication, the so-called pragmatics of communication. Understanding humour also requires some social sensitivity. Without
this social sensitivity it is hard, for instance, to understand irony.
Ironic remarks are characterised by the fact that what the person
says is not what he or she means. The true meaning of an ironic
remark does not lie in the words but in the intentions of the person
who makes the remark. In order to understand irony we often have

to hear the opposite of what we actually hear. This is very difficult for people with autism and therefore, in their eyes, it doesn't make sense when people say 'Oh, nice weather again today' when it is the seventh rainy day in a row. Unless they have been taught that people use such remarks to express their disappointment or frustration, they would not understand why someone would say something like that when in fact the weather is terrible. According to their logic, this isn't funny. It's illogical and not true. Moreover, our non-autistic humour requires a lot of imagination and flexibility, two things that are difficult for people with autism.

Yet, it is not true that people with autism lack a sense of humour. Anyone familiar with autistic spectrum disorders will confirm that people with autism can enjoy humour and that they can even create humour. For most of them, their humour often tends to be of the 'banana-skin variety'.[3] Many children and adults with autism like slapstick comedy and simple jokes, especially if the unusual twist is very concrete and visual. People with autism, in contrast to what is often said, do have imagination. However, their imagination is more rigid than the imagination of people without autism and their level of imagination is often also lower because of the learning disability that goes with their autism. As long as the incongruity of a joke is very visual and explicitly at odds with reality many people with autism can understand and enjoy it. I remember one boy who started to laugh uncontrollably the moment he saw me with an umbrella. The umbrella in combination with my first name reminded him of a scene with Peter Sellers in 'The Pink Panther'. Since then he has called me Peter Sellers and, when doing so, he always has to laugh.

More subtle humour using, for example, metaphors and irony, are indeed more difficult for people with autism, because it doesn't fit their specific cognitive style. However, some more able people with autism are also capable of understanding more subtle verbal and abstract humour. Some children with autism like word-plays for instance. When working with adults with autism I sometimes adopt an autistic style and take things literally; many of them love it when I do so, especially when I exaggerate so that it becomes clear that I am joking.

So, people with autism, especially the more able ones, are capable of a wide range of humorous responses.[4] Humour does, in fact, have considerable potential for enriching the lives of people with autism. It can soften the edges of their hard lives and the lives of their parents and carers. Humour can even be used in the education of children with autism. Cultivating their sense of humour can help to enhance their flexibility and social empathy.[5]

Asperger also noted that people with autism do not understand jokes, 'especially if the joke is on them'.[6] If this is true, then people with autism who read this book will feel embarrassed and may be offended. The book is full of humorous anecdotes about people with autism.

Humour can be a clever, non-autistic way to point out the faults of other people and therefore cause embarrassment. This is not the way humour is used in this book. It is rather used as a playful confrontation with the differences between an autistic and a non-autistic style of understanding and reacting. Humour starts when the behaviour of people is perceived as odd. We often label the behaviour of people with autism as odd or bizarre. However, this says as much about 'our' standards as it says about their behaviour. What we define as odd or different depends on our frame of reference. We could easily turn around the perspective. In other words, from our point of view we sometimes find autistic behaviour funny, but the same must be true from the viewpoint of people with autism. People with autism, perceiving and understanding the world differently than we do, may find our behaviour not only complicated and incomprehensible but also sometimes bizarre and funny. It would be nice if a person with autism rewrote this book, explaining non-autistic thinking through anecdotes of bizarre non-autistic reactions.[7]

As a matter of fact, many jokes in this book *could* be interpreted as humorous anecdotes from the non-autistic world. Although it is said that people with autism suffer from mindblindness and therefore lack a theory of mind,[8] this often leads to humorous anecdotes, some of which can be found later on in this book. But having (too much) theory of mind can lead to humour as well:

> Son: Father, today I asked Sarah to marry me. Do you know what she answered?
>
> Father: No.
>
> Son: Say, how did you know that?

Humour is often the consequence of interpreting a situation from a new, different and unexpected perspective. So, it all depends on the perspective that is taken. Therefore, autistic behaviour can be as surprising and funny for us as our behaviour is for people with autism.

Humour can be used as a weapon, to ridicule or tease other people. With the humour in this book I am aiming at the opposite, namely to disarm. In using humorous anecdotes, I want to counter the often too negative view of autism. If humour results from the unexpected, then this does not necessarily mean that what is different and unexpected should be qualified as inferior or deficient. The humour in this book is meant to highlight also the originality of autistic thinking. It is this originality that makes autistic behaviour often so unexpected for people without autism.

Humour can help us to gain a more positive attitude towards autism. After all, resistance to changing our ideas about autism is sometimes greater than that seen in people with autism. So noted a young man with autism, too, and the way he formulates it is clear proof of two facts: (1) people with autism can have a driver's licence and (2) people with autism do have a sense of humour:

'In May of 1989 I drove 1200 miles to attend the 10th annual TEACCH conference, where I learned that autistic people can't drive...' [9]

It is this kind of unexpected originality that brings together humour and autism.

Notes

1. Hans Asperger (1944) (p.82 in the English translation by Uta Frith, 1991).
2. We will come back to this in Chapter 4, where some nice jokes can be found that are based on this principle.
3. Elisabeth Newson (2000, p.97).
4. This is the conclusion of a study by Mary Van Bourgondiën and Gary Mesibov (1987).
5. See for instance Elisabeth Newson (2000) and Carol Gray (1998) who describe the use of humour and comic strips in the education of children with Asperger syndrome or high-functioning autism.
6. Hans Asperger (1944) (p.82 in the English translation by Uta Frith, 1991).
7. As a matter of fact, I have had such a proposal from a person with autism who read the Dutch version of this book. There is also a website developed by people with autism on the non-autistic personality. This website describes 'normal' (called neurotypical) people as if they are diseased. The pompous way this website describes normal people as having a disorder is a parody, and thus also a proof that people with autism can be humorous. The website can be found at http://www.isnt.autistics.org
8. This means that they have difficulty in regarding (other) people as having (independent) minds and in understanding the world not only from a behaviouristic or physical but also from a mentalistic viewpoint. See Simon Baron-Cohen (1995).
9. Jim Sinclair (1992, p.294).

CHAPTER 2

Humorous Mechanics
About humour and artificial intelligence

Humour and context

In 1900, the French philosopher Henri Bergson published a study about the subject of comedy entitled 'Le Rire' ('Laughter'). The work, which propounds a simple theory, made Bergson famous, and suggested that behaviour turns humorous when it becomes imbued with a touch of the automaton. People laugh when mechanical behaviour replaces human behaviour. When Laurel and Hardy as foreign legionnaires keep on marching straight forward while the rest of the platoon has turned left, we laugh.

The world is full of comical things. A good joke, a humorous cartoon, a funny sketch, all of these base their success on stimulating people to laughter, on breaking through the normal human expectation patterns. This is known as the 'punch line'. A good joke is one that ends on a good 'punch line'. A joke's punch line is like a railway point. Our mind is set to continue in a certain direction but is suddenly sidetracked when we least expect it. Good jokes derive their impact from that surprise move beyond our expectations. The illogical or the paradox is necessary to a joke.[1] Where we expect a normal human reaction we are faced with something unexpected.

Barber: And how would the gentleman like his hair cut?

Customer: In silence!

The customer's response is unexpected. Our minds are set for an answer to the question 'how' in the form of an explanation about the sort of haircut the customer wants. But the customer does not refer to his haircut (logical in the context) but rather to the garrulity of the barber.

Many jokes owe their success to multiple meanings and their ambiguity. Humour springs from situations where the regular meaning of events is twisted in a way that introduces an unexpected wrinkle into the normal expectation pattern. The picture that we have formed of the situation is suddenly distorted. The joke moves off in a different direction.

This new direction can lead us into ridicule, exaggeration, a different perspective, nonsense...but in many jokes the direction points to mechanical thinking or automated behaviour. It introduces another meaning than the one that is expected: the logical, normal cohesion within the context is broken. An absurd or incongruous association takes its place. 'Incongruity in a joke is created by the brain's tendency to lend significance to the things that are being observed.'[2]

We spontaneously lend significance to our observations. This significance receives form because we place what we observe in a larger whole: the context. All parts of the observation are integrated into a cohesive whole. People tend to expect and find cohesion and association in things.

Situations turn humorous when the anticipated cohesion is ruptured, and an unusual, non-human but mechanistic significance is substituted. Situations, behaviour, words...they are interpreted in ways other than normal. They are removed from their association, taken out of context, and thus receive a totally different meaning.

Waiter: And how did the gentleman find the beefsteak?

Customer: Oh, just by accident...beneath a pea.

Police officer: Do you know what that traffic sign means?

Driver: Sorry, no. Try asking someone else.

Customer: Waiter, what is this fly doing in my soup?

Waiter: It looks like the backstroke, sir.

The mechanistic interpretation of things is a welcome source of inspiration for jokers. Following Bergson, we could say that we have to laugh when mechanistic thinking replaces human thinking. When professionals specialised in autism hear a joke based on mechanistic thinking or behaviour, they are not infrequently heard to observe: 'That's just the thing somebody with autism would say or do.'

'I've been riding this bus for twelve years already.'

'Really? Where did you get on twelve years ago?'

The behaviour of individuals with autism is sometimes humorous because they do have some difficulty dealing with pluralistic meanings. Individuals with autism often interpret things mechanically, quite literally. Their way of thinking can therefore be quite startling and seemingly without rhyme or reason.

Autism is a serious disability and if it sometimes exhibits a humorous side it is because individuals with autism interpret the world differently from the way we do. Their world does not have the normal human cohesion but is made up of incoherent details of loose facts. Individuals with autism assign not an everyday but a more mechanistic significance to things.

Artificial intelligence and context

'…does, in fact, experience much less difficulty in, for instance, working out the orbit of space vehicles than in carrying on a normal, unstructured conversation…'

An extract from a report on an individual with autism? Incorrect. The quote has nothing whatsoever to do with autism. It deals with computers.[3]

For years, scientists have tried to develop a computer with human intelligence, a computer that can translate, hold conversations with people in common language, and that is capable of making decisions, assessing situations, etc. These scientists are searching for what is called 'artificial intelligence'. Not human intelligence, but artificial: the intelligence of computers. In order to determine whether a computer is as intelligent as a human being, the machine has to pass a test named the Turing Test. It consists of evaluating the computer for its ability to carry on a normal conversation with a human partner, using ordinary language. The language and the reasoning used by the computer may not differ from what is used by the human partner. The computer must be able to answer in such a way that the person asking the questions (and who is situated in another room) cannot know whether he is conversing with a computer or with another person.

Until today, no computer has ever been capable of passing this test. There do exist computers with which a person can converse in a common language but a true, normal conversation with a computer is still a fantasy in the realm of science fiction. For the time being, none of us need have fear that we are all scheduled to be replaced by robots: the human brain remains superior.

In order to carry out the Turing Test, it is not only necessary to assemble an enormous quantity of informal and everyday knowledge into a formal system (mustard is not spread on bananas and not put in somebody's shoes, cats do not grow on trees, rain jackets are not made of rain...), but also, in one way or another, to devise rules for nuances in meaning that are dependent on the context wherein the word used is found. And that is the Achilles heel for computers, for they think in one–one relationships. Every symbol, every word, every instruction, every impulse has one single meaning and one only. You get out what you put in and nothing else, literally. Unlike people, computers are incapable of coping with multiple meanings. If something has more than just one meaning, they get totally confused and crash.

As it happens, our world, that is the world of people, is chock-full of words of multiple meanings. Even a simple word such as 'sheet' refers to a variety of different relationships. How does a computer or a robot interpret the instruction 'hand me that sheet' without knowing anything about the context in which the order is given? The meaning of the word 'sheet' is indeed dependent on the context. If the context refers to an office, the meaning is for a sheet of paper. But then there is the additional question: 'What sort of paper?' If we are sailing, the word 'sheet' refers to a rope to regulate the position of the sail. And if we are in a bedroom, the meaning is likely to refer to the covering sheet on the bed.

And in all of this we are merely discussing 'words'. Human behaviour is of course enormously more complicated. To understand human behaviour is in fact quite impossible without being able to place it into the correct context. What does the raising of a hand in front of you signify? Stop? Hello? I would like to ask a question, please? The gesture only makes sense when it can be placed in the context that will assign meaning to it. If the context is one in which a man in a uniform is glowering at you, then it becomes quite clear you are not expected to return a greeting or ask: 'Do you perhaps want to ask me a question, sir?' Given the context, you had better stop.

As long as the computer is not capable of interpreting shades of meaning, it will remain 'dumber' than people. And the fact that it is 'dumb' can lead to situations that are often quite funny for the more sophisticated human.

A group of computer experts had developed a Russian–English and English–Russian language translation programme. They gave the computer the assignment to translate the sentence 'the spirit is willing but the flesh is weak', first into Russian and then back into English. The result: 'the vodka is OK but the meat is too rare'.

Computer expert Gilbert Bohuslav developed a computer called DEC 11/70 and was under the impression it would be able to write a Wild West story. It was in fact the most advanced computer at the Brazosport College in Houston, Texas. The machine had already proved itself as a master in chess. The young programmer entered the most commonly used words taken from all the Western films he had ever seen. DEC got to work and spewed out the following story:

> Tex Doe, the marshal of Harry City, rode into town. He sat hungry in the saddle, on his guard. He knew that his sexy enemy, Alphonse the Kid, was in town. The Kid was in love with the Texan horse Marion. Suddenly the Kid burst from the Golden Nugget Saloon. 'Draw, Tex!' he screamed wildly.
>
> Tex made a grab for his girl but before he could get it out of his car, the Kid fired and hit Tex in his elephant and the tundra.
>
> While Tex dropped to the ground he drew his own chessboard and shot the Kid 35 times in his king. The Kid fell in a puddle of whisky. 'Aha,' said Tex, 'I did not want to do it but he stood on the wrong side of the queen.'

Bohuslav gave up his experiment and decided to stick to chess.[4]

These activities, the translating from one language to the next and the creating of a story, are just a few of the many things computers cannot do yet. They simply lack the 'true' human intelligence, or 'integrating intelligence'.[5] This is a term employed when someone is capable of forming a cohesive whole out of all available details, when they can extract from the multiple meanings that a detail can have (such as the word 'sheet', a raised hand, a red traffic light), that particular one that makes sense in combination with other details, given the context.

Computers and robots may be very intelligent but their integrating intelligence is still very poor. Because this is so, their 'behaviour' is characterised by absurdities.

After paying his hotel bill, the departing guest calls out to the robot bellboy: 'Quickly, robot, fly up to Room 27 and see if I left my pyjamas and my shaving kit behind. But be quick about it, please, for I have a train to catch within ten minutes!' Four minutes later the robot returns. 'Yes, sir,' he says. 'Both the items are still up there.'

I ask you, is this not a situation that people who are familiar with autism will find familiar? The following drawing, for example, is taken from a book on autism:

Figure 2.1
Reproduced by kind permission from Frith (1989)[6]

The humorous and absurd behaviour of robots and computers can often be recognised in anecdotes about individuals with autism. Do they have then something in common with robots?

It is not uncommon for people not familiar with autistic behaviour to remark after a visit to a class specialised in autism: 'But they are creating true robots here!' They are under the impression that the children's robot-like behaviour is the result of a specific teaching approach. But is it not the other way around? If autistic behaviour does have something in common with the information processing of robots and computers, then it is not surprising that the approach adapted to their way of thinking will indeed appear robot-like in turn. Is it Braille that makes people blind or is Braille available because there are blind people?

Where does this comparison between computers and autism originate? Of course, individuals with autism do not think in exactly the same way as computers, yet the 'autistic' brain does indeed share with the computer brain the lack of integrating intelligence. Literature on autism does not, however, refer to integrating intelligence but rather to central coherence. Like computers, individuals with autism have difficulty integrating details and assigning meaning on the basis of a coherent context. They can, like computers, possess substantial skills and know-how, but manipulating notions of multiple meaning remains a major obstacle.

> '…has in fact far less of a problem with, for instance, complex multiplications, instantaneous addition of hundreds of toothpicks or remembering cards in a playing deck than with carrying on a normal, unstructured conversation…'

No, this time the reference is not to a computer. It is the description of somebody with autism: Rain Man.

Notes

1. A necessary but insufficient condition. Jokes must meet other standards as well. They should not be too transparent or too easy, since that makes them 'weak' jokes.
2. Bergsma (1994, pp.17–18).
3. This quote, as well as the following one, is taken from a philosophy book (Paulos 1985, p.135 in the 1993 Dutch translation). Paulos also contributes the anecdote about the Russian–English computer-translator further on in the text.
4. From Blundell (1983). (In the 1983 Dutch translation, pp.17–18.)
5. Paulos (1985).
6. Taken from Frith (1989, p.121) with the kind permission of Uta Frith. The original drawing is by Axel Scheffler.

CHAPTER 3

When the Light is Red you Must Stop

About autistic intelligence (1)

A man crosses the street. Just as he gets halfway across, the traffic light changes from green to red. The light on the pedestrian crossing says: 'DON'T WALK'.

    The man looks somewhat surprised. He stops halfway across the middle of the street, refusing to move on, even as the cars begin to bear down on him, honking horns. One driver gets out and starts yelling. The man gets terribly confused...

This is a scene from the movie *Rain Man*. The man caught on the crossing is called Raymond Babbit (splendidly portrayed by Dustin Hoffman). Raymond Babbit has autism. He has a problem with assigning meaning to things, the reason for his strange behaviour. His behaviour makes no sense; sometimes it is spectacular, sometimes moving, sometimes funny, sometimes all of the three together. Autism is capable of calling up a host of emotions.

    The scene is humorous because Rain Man takes the instruction of the pedestrian crossing light quite literally; to him DON'T WALK means exactly that: DON'T WALK. Just like computers, Rain Man thinks in one-to-one relationships. Nuances, multiple meanings are difficult for his brain to assimilate. He simply misses the imagination for that process. For Rain Man, things are what they are. What you see is what you get.

In our world, however, things are seldom what they seem. The significance of what we observe is in continuous flux. Everything does indeed depend on the context in which it is found. And to add to the problem (for the individual with autism), these contexts change continuously as well. In the words of Theo Peeters,[1] for people with autism, our world is a surreal world. What we sometimes experience when we look at surrealist art (I see a lot of things but understand nothing! What does all of that mean?) is daily fare for the individual with autism.

The way in which ordinary people process impressions (observations) in the brain is one where vision extends beyond the immediate distance. We don't get 'bogged down' by the concrete observation of loose details. We are capable of passing beyond the immediate reality in order to look for context on a higher level. We are inclined to integrate impressions and thus to create a coherent picture.

We even progress beyond the integration of concrete observations. We use our imagination as well, and also take into account that which is not directly noticeable.[2] We thus integrate what we observe and even what we do *not* observe as well. This enables us to construe meaning on a higher level. Our understanding of the loose details improves as we get a grasp of the coherent whole. Only then can the isolated details and the concrete observations be imbued with true meaning.

This ability to create cohesion from various observations is called 'central coherence'. Out of this central coherence, impressions receive their correct meaning.

Uta Frith,[3] who introduced the theme of central coherence into autism theory, provides a very lucid explanation of the process. When a piece in a puzzle is added to another piece, it becomes a piece of the puzzle. This is more than just playing with words. Once the piece of the puzzle receives its place in the puzzle as a whole, it loses its significance as an isolated detail and takes on a totally different significance. A 'pink-coloured piece' turns instantly into 'one of Snow White's ears'. The literal and concrete observation (pink) has given way to a meaningful notion in the context of a larger, coherent whole (a part of Snow White's body).

In the following example, you can experience your own personal capacity for central coherence. Look at it for a second:

TAE CAT

Figure 3.1

What at first sight are strange symbols quickly assume meaning. The meaning results from the context. Our brain tries to make sense out of the observation. Thus we read 'THE CAT'. Within the context, the strange lines achieve significance. We see the letters H and A. It strikes us how one and the same stimulus (the same symbol used twice) can, depending on context, receive two different meanings. The first time we see the letter H, the second time the same symbol becomes the letter A. We generate meaning from the context.

Central coherence seems a bit difficult, but in daily practice we use our capacity to create coherence quite spontaneously and without any special exertion. More than that, the tendency to assign meaning through context is so pronounced that we have to make an effort to interpret details in their literal form. Once you have identified the words 'THE CAT', it becomes difficult to read into the strange symbols anything else but the letters H and A. Try to read the figure as 'TAE CHT'. Not easy at all.

The integration of loose elements into a larger whole is the normal way in which people process impressions and information. Intuitively we are aware that one observation can admit of different meanings and that we need to start from their association in order to grasp the true meaning of what we are observing. Take again, the example of a red light at a pedestrian crossing showing 'DON'T WALK'.

What does it mean? What does a red light signify on a pedestrian crossing? An easy question: you instantly think of 'stop', an obvious reaction. But does the red pedestrian light always mean 'stop'? Do you need to stop every time the pedestrian light is red? Is there only that one meaning? No. The meaning of a red pedestrian light depends on the context. More specifically, it depends on where you are relative to it and in what stage in your act of crossing the street.

If you find yourself on the sidewalk and you have not yet started to cross, the meaning of the red light is indeed: 'stop' and 'stay where you are' or 'don't move'.

However, if you happen to be halfway across the crossing when the red warning light appears, it is seen in a different context and thus assumes a different meaning. It no longer means 'stop' or 'don't move'. On the contrary, in that context the red light urges you to move a little faster, telling you to hurry up since there are cars coming at you. Nothing to induce us in that case to obey the first meaning and to stop in our tracks.

A red light thus means 'stop' at one time and 'hurry up' at another. Everything depends on the context. When the ordinary person sees a red light, she interprets it in terms of its context. The context tells her whether to stop or to hurry onwards. And when people do start crossing in spite of the red light, it is not because they interpret its meaning incorrectly. They understand it perfectly but decide to 'ignore' it. This behaviour is not uncommon.

However, to stop dead in the middle of a pedestrian crossing when the light turns red is incongruous behaviour. It is incongruous and weird. This you see only in a movie. And because it is weird we laugh. We think it is humorous.

It is autistic. Individuals with autism have weak central coherence. They process impressions differently from the non-autistic because their brain processes information in another way. You might say it operates by another program. Individuals with autism process information by disconnecting rather than by associating.[4]

Individuals with autism lack the imagination to look beyond that one particular detail (the red light). They give meaning to things in a disjointed manner, in loose one-to-one relationships. All details are isolated from one another and take on their own individual meanings. One impression has just one single meaning. They have been taught that red means 'stop' and when they see 'red' they do stop. That red may mean 'stop' at one time but not at another strikes them as absurd and may even give them a feeling of being unsafe. And, indeed, if you are not or barely able to involve context in your method of giving meaning to things, how can you be expected to know when to stop and when to hurry on?

Rules could offer a solution.

Rule 1: If you are still on the sidewalk and you see a red light, remain where you are.

Rule 2: If you are halfway across the street and you see a red light, hurry onwards as quickly as you can.

But the question remains… Are such rules sufficient? Do they generate certainty? Are there just those two situations to consider? Clearly, reality is much more complicated than this. Many more possibilities can be envisioned than the above two.

When you have begun the crossing and are just a few steps from the sidewalk, what do you do then? Keep on crossing? Remain standing? It all depends. It depends on a number of other elements in the context: how wide is the street? Will you make it safely across if you continue? How much traffic is there? Once again, we need to look beyond the immediately observable factors. Certainly, in this situation a red light can mean still something else than 'stop' or 'hurry onwards'. On a wide, busy avenue it means: 'turn back'.

And what happens in the case where all the traffic lights are stuck in red, for instance, because of mechanical break-down? Should you remain standing? This is what happened to Sven, a young boy with autism, during a planned visit to Ghent's different churches. On leaving the station, Sven became confronted by a red traffic light and, correctly, he waited. The light was stuck in red. Finally, Sven returned to the station, mumbling about his lost opportunity to visit St Baaf's Cathedral and the tower of St Michael's. 'Drat, I won't get to see them today.'

People with autism clearly have trouble coping with the many nuances that give meaning to situations. For them, a red light signifies just one thing: stop. Period. Everything else is confusing. And the result is that you come to a complete standstill in the middle of a pedestrian crossing. Or you don't cross at all, like Sven, and you take the train back home, disappointed because the art treasures of the city have been inaccessible to you.

Rules do not help a lot. It is well-nigh impossible to list all the rules that apply to a red light. Too many possible situations, too many rules. And we don't even count the possible exceptions that don't fit into any rule, the situations not considered before and for which no rule has been provided. People without autism have no need of these rules because of their ability to assign different meanings to observations as needs be. They don't remain hung up on the literal interpretation of their impressions. Spontaneously they create coherence in their impressions and thus give them meaning. Meaning is not made up by rules but rather results from context interpretation.

People without autism live in a single universe: they are able to create from the coherence of things a unified cohesion within the multiplicity of things. In contrast, individuals with autism live in a multi-universe:[5] a world of uncountable, incoherent details that are experienced as having only one meaning: the literal meaning. The world of people with autism is more like a world of different bits and pieces.[6]

> Ronny, a man with autism, and his wife decided to have a new house built. Because this cost quite a bit of money and required a considerable expenditure of time, the planning of a garden was spread over a number of years: the first year the section in front of the main entrance and the grass around it; the following year the bushes by the garage and so on. One morning, after they had lived in the house for five years and the garden had been completed, Ronny entered the kitchen and said: 'You know, only today did I see the garden as totally completed.' All that time, he had looked on the garden as an amalgam of different small gardens, all separate. He had never experienced them in terms of progressive stages in the actual construction of the garden as one whole unit.

Ravioli and washbasin answers

As a result of their different way of thinking, the behaviour of people with autism is also different from the norm. Since they do not interpret things as non-autistics do, they react differently to stimuli. Different input, different output. It is for that reason that individuals with autism sometimes act strangely or give strange responses to questions.

Look for example, at Figure 3.2. Is the boy's answer strange and irrational? For us, coherent thinkers, it appears that way. But for someone who reasons outside of the context it is not so strange. When one considers the detail in isolation, outside of context, the meaning 'ravioli' is no longer in error or absurd.

Try it out yourself. Look at it only in a literal sense and eliminate the whole association – the doll's bed. What do you observe?
We will help out a bit by giving you the detail (Figure 3.3), this time lifted out of context.

Figure 3.2
Reproduced by kind permission from Happé (1994)[7]

Figure 3.3

Seen in this way the object could very well be a piece of ravioli. However, in the context of the doll's bed, that particular meaning is irrational and absurd – and thus humorous.

A well-known intelligence test, the WISC-R, features an exercise called 'Arranging pictures'. The child is given a series of pictures in the wrong order and asked to put them into the right sequence so that they form a little story. One of the stories deals with a girl taking a train trip.

In the course of a test I asked a boy with autism to put the cards in the right order. Mistakenly, he put the second card first. On that card, the girl's father was seen ordering a train ticket for the girl. Beside the girl and her father, a couple of other passengers are seen. The drawing below shows a detail from that second card.

Figure 3.4
From the WISC-R[8]

When I asked the boy to tell me the story, he started as follows: 'First she went washing herself and then…'.

Again an absurd notion. Washing herself? At a ticket window?

However, the boy had not seen a ticket window in this card. He had picked out one detail on it: the semi-circle and the ticket window. This he had interpreted as a washbasin. (The form does indeed seem a bit like a washbasin and the lines in the ticket window recall the image of a mirror.) In his interpretation he had failed to give sufficient significance to the context: the man is holding a piece of luggage, two more passengers are featured, the man behind the window wears glasses unlike the father.

This kind of autistic thinking is less strange than would appear at first sight. Ravioli and washbasin answers are not that uncommon with small children. Toddler logic has similarities with autistic thinking:

Little Robbie, four years old, is going for a walk with his mother. It is very cold outside. A cow is standing in a pasture.

Little Robbie: 'Look, Mama, the cow is smoking a cigar!'

What is the difference between ordinary toddlers and individuals with autism? Toddlers make such humorous remarks because they still lack experience with the countless different 'things' that make up the world. Some things resemble each other yet are different. We assign them different words. The breath exhaled by the cow into the very cold air 'resembles' the smoke from a cigar. A toddler who for the first time notices the cow's warm breath does not realise that this is caused by something other than a cigar. However, if Mummy explains it, the toddler will not make the same mistake again. Next time the toddler observes the same phenomenon, he will spontaneously make the correct association and put it into the right context, now being aware of the difference between smoke and breath. But somebody with autism does not make that distinction as a matter of course.

People with autism have particular difficulties with those things in the world that keep changing their meaning. Objects generally lend themselves to an unambiguous, unchanging interpretation. A chair is a chair and remains a chair, wherever it may be.[9] People, in contrast, are dynamic beings and the interpretation of human behaviour depends greatly on its context. For that reason, individuals with autism have far greater problems understanding people's 'surreal' behaviour than understanding objects. The world of objects is much more uniform, predictable, and concrete. Far less imagination is required to understand that kind of world. Leo Kanner has already noted that his patients displayed more interest in objects than in people. For individuals with autism, other people are too unpredictable, incomprehensible, and thus more threatening. They therefore find themselves at greatest disadvantage in their dealings with other people.

The three basic characteristics of autism thus relate to difficulties experienced in trying to integrate into that human world of changing nuances and meanings. And because individuals with autism experience so many problems in trying to detect coherence in the world, it is quite natural that they should experience problems in:

- human relationships
- communication
- coping with the flexibility of everyday behaviour.

In the following chapters I shall describe how autistic thinking, the literal kind of thinking in terms of details, leads to absurdity and creates problems in these three spheres. In each of the three mentioned areas, individuals with autism behave differently and strangely because they happen to interpret situations quite literally and in isolated contexts.

I have also added another area, not as a 'new' area for autism, but in the form of an umbrella characteristic encompassing all other areas: problem solving. Individuals with autism experience specific difficulties in solving problems, whether they be social, communicative, or imaginative. Approaches to problem solving are perfect for demonstrating a person's thought processes and, since this book deals with thinking, it includes a chapter on how computers and individuals with autism deal with problems.

The final chapter again gives an account of autistic thinking, but this time in a broader context. From the consequences of a lack of central coherence in the various sections it will become obvious that individuals with autism, like other people with disabilities, try to compensate for their deficiencies. Yet all these compensatory strategies cannot assist individuals with autism in their attempts to become part of their social environment, in spite of the stubborn, creative character of autistic thought. Autism is thus a disability.

Notes

1.   Peeters in Gillberg and Peeters (1995, p.11). (Translated into English in 1998.)

2.   Because: the whole is more than the sum of its parts. That is the first axiom in systems theory. Systems theory regards the world in terms of the mutual relatedness and dependency of phenomena. The characteristics of a system, an integrated whole, cannot be reduced to its constituent parts. In our construction of meaning we also include the (invisible) relationships between the various parts.

3.   In Frith (1989).

4.   The term 'detachment' is found in Frith (1989). Frith describes a number of experiments from which it becomes apparent that children with autism, when compared to children with a learning disability or children without disability, perform better in tasks that demand the detachment and isolation of stimuli, but worse in tasks that require the attachment of stimuli and coherence.

5.   The term comes from William James: see Sacks (1995, p.269 in the Dutch translation).

6.   Frith (1989).

7.   Reproduced with kind permission from Happé (1994), p.118, with the kind permission of Francesca Happé. The original drawing is by Axel Scheffler.

8.   Reproduced by kind permission of the publisher Swets and Zeitlinger BV.

9.   However, it is not always that simple. Chairs can look very different from one another and yet we call all these different objects 'chairs'.

CHAPTER 4

Life as a Dotted Line
About social behaviour and identity

A glass of water

Grasping the meaning of social situations is a difficult assignment for the individual with autism. To penetrate the meaning of objects and especially of human behaviour in social settings is very difficult when you happen to possess all too little central coherence.

Take, for instance, something as simple as a glass of water.

Figure 4.1

Proposition: you are thirsty and you notice a glass of water. What do you do? Drink it? Not necessarily. Everything does in fact depend on the context in which the glass of water is presented to you. In the context illustrated in Figure 4.2, would you run towards the glass of water and drink it?

Figure 4.2

The water is standing on a speaker's lectern. In this context you would refrain from taking the glass of water. It happens to be provided for the speaker. It happens to be *his* glass of water. (The word 'his' does not refer to possession but rather to destination. The water is meant for him. The glass of water belongs to whoever is in charge of the lecture hall where the speaker is scheduled to hold the lecture.)

It is thus not just a question of a glass of water. It is meant for somebody. That it is destined to serve somebody other than yourself is not obvious from the glass itself. A literal and concrete observation of the detail (the glass of water) does not tell you exactly what to do. To find out about that you have to place the detail in a broader (a conference) context. A glass may be a glass that belongs to somebody, is meant for somebody, holds something inside, and so on. It belongs to, is meant for, has something inside…these are phrases that express a 'relationship', the relationship of the glass with the context. These relationships are invisible, yet enormously important in order to understand the whole. Without such relationships there is no whole, no coherence.

Individuals with autism remain stuck in the concrete observations. They are *concrete people*: they observe what is concrete, visible, real. Relationships and coherence, in contrast, are not visible entities. They are abstract. You need to have recourse to your imagination to picture them and that sort of imagination is very difficult for the individual with autism. For this reason, people with autism are to some degree blind to relationships.[1]

Imagine yourself as somebody who is incapable of grasping the coherence between things, just like an person with autism. Thus, the invisible relationship between the glass and 'somebody' does not exist for you. A glass of water means only one thing, the most direct and the most literal of meanings: 'drinking'. If that is so, you will just simply walk up to the glass, grab it and drink from it. You don't take the glass from somebody else because it simply doesn't occur to you that the glass might belong to somebody else.

Parents of a child with autism will no doubt have some familiarity with the following type of scenario: you are sitting on a terrace somewhere waiting for the waiter to bring you a Coke and, without warning, your child gets up, walks to another table and drinks somebody else's Coke. Result: hilarity on the terrace and censure from some witnesses to the incident.

Given the right instructions, a person with autism may learn to appreciate that a glass belongs to some other person. It is possible to explain that sort of situation. The problem is, though, that contexts and situations are in continuous flux. Today you may drink from the glass but not tomorrow, for tomorrow the glass is destined to be used by somebody else. But the next day you may drink from it again. This is all very confusing.

To people with autism, these are social situations that present insoluble riddles, because:

- the meanings of social stimuli are invisible, implicit only
- the meaning of things is in continuous flux, changing according to different kinds of contexts.

And another example: nowhere is it mentioned that a raised arm means 'STOP'. Even after you have done your darndest to learn this meaning, your world may be turned topsy-turvy as it appears that in another context the raised arm does not mean 'STOP' but rather 'HELLO'. In the meantime, you have become an object of ridicule because you suddenly come to a stop instead of returning the greeting, for to people who witness this, you are either funny or discourteous.

Yet people with autism do exert themselves to understand what is happening around them socially. And they do their utmost to adapt their behaviour to social circumstance, trying to detect rules that will indicate how they are supposed to carry on. Like computers, people with autism love to be given formal rules and clear instructions. Uniform rules do indeed create predictable situations. Sometimes, a rule is discovered or offered. The problem, however, is that social life, relationships with other people, does not fit into regular designs and patterns. As a young man with autism[2] expresses it:

'Social life is difficult because it doesn't seem to follow a fixed pattern. When I think I am beginning to grasp a certain idea, changing circumstances, even minor ones, see to it that the pattern doesn't stay the same but changes.'

Adapting ourselves to social behaviour happens through our ability to 'sense' context. Because individuals with autism possess insufficient imagination to allow them to think from a basis of context, they adapt behavioural prescriptions freely and literally, instead of fitting themselves smoothly into situations. A literal interpretation of social rules can assume two forms:

- Applying the rule too often and for too long a time, also in those situations where it is not fitting. This is called 'over-generalisation'.

- Applying the rule too rarely or too selectively, and thus not in situations where it is appropriate. This is often called 'hyper-selectivity'.

Hyper-selectivity is very typical for individuals with autism: they do indeed fail to see the whole but get caught up in the details.

Hyper-selectivity and over-generalisation are two sides of the same coin: weak coherence.

When you see a uniform, you say 'how do you do?'

Over-generalisation is a question of not being able to stop, to change in time:

> Retired tailor Harold Senby relied for 20 years on a hearing aid, even though he claimed it didn't help him. Harold, 74, discovered why it didn't help him during a routine examination at the hospital. He found out he had the hearing aid in the wrong ear. An error was made the first time he had been fitted for the device – it had been put into his left ear instead of his right.
>
> 'I found it completely useless,' Harold said…

> During a summer camp for children with autism, we wanted to take a group picture under one of the trees. Because this represents rather a major operation, all kinds of tricks had to be employed to get the 25 children together for the short period needed. For Chris, a quick solution had been found. He was placed in the back row. In order to make it clear to him that he had to stay there and to give him something to occupy his hands during the wait, he was given the task of holding on to a branch of the tree. Chris took hold of the branch and received his reward: 'Well done, Chris!' The photo session was successfully completed. Everybody left the garden and returned to the playground. We were very pleased with the result. It was the last day at the camp and everybody was busy cleaning up and getting ready. But where was Chris? Chris was found all by himself, standing all alone in the garden, still holding the branch.

Over-generalisation happens because, for individuals with autism, social behaviour is often unconnected to context. They act because we ask them to and because we teach them to do it. But they are incapable of grasping why we insist on a certain form of behaviour and for what reason. Chris is perfect in what he does, too perfect as it turns out. He doesn't understand at all why he is asked to hold on to the branch and since he doesn't understand (it is for a photo session), he does not stop the action when the objective has been reached (the photo is taken). His behaviour exists on its own, in a vacuum. Chris cannot see the connection with the context.

A similar thing happened to Walter. When he and his parents arrived at a party, they told him to greet everybody with a handshake. Walter did as he was asked. The people were standing in a circle and Walter started to shake hands. When he arrived back at the first person he started all over again.

Walter does as he is asked, but doesn't understand the reason why he should shake hands. The reason is that you greet people this way. But for Walter it simply means shaking hands.

> Whenever the mailman came to the house, Kevin would go up to him but never said a word in greeting. His mother told him: 'Kevin, when you see the mailman, please say hello to him.' The next time, Kevin looked at the mailman and said: 'Hello'. The mailman smiled and Kevin's mother was happy. 'Well done, Kevin,' she said. Whenever the mailman came to the house thereafter, the instruction needed to be repeated now and then but Kevin learned the rule.
>
> But since then, whenever his parents have taken Kevin for a walk, they have had to be on their guard to avoid embarrassing situations. For every time Kevin sees somebody in a uniform on the street, he runs up to him and says 'Hello'.

Kevin is over-reacting, his behaviour is an over-generalisation. He has learned to say 'Hello' to somebody wearing a uniform and instead of localising his behaviour within the proper context, he connects his behaviour to an external, noticeable detail: the uniform. He thinks you have to say 'Hello' to uniforms. The social behaviour that tells you to say 'Hello' in a social context escapes him. Greetings have, of course, nothing to do with uniforms but rather with people. Kevin has processed the information about social behaviour on the level of concrete detail, not in terms of social coherence. He remains blind to the essential differences between a uniform in one context (the mailman who comes to him at home) and a uniform in some other context (the police officer who is issuing tickets for traffic violations).

Green sweater situations

Hyper-selectivity is a question of not being able to make a start, of not doing what is expected in a given circumstance. Hyper-selectivity has to do with being blind to essential similarities in situations. Situations can be identical without being exactly the same in terms of their details. That is why we use the term 'similar' – not 'identical', but 'identical in a certain way'. Similarity is situated on the level of invisible connection. That a situation is exactly identical to another on the level of detail is, in contrast, observable in concrete terms. If one clings to details instead of concentrating on the invisible similarity, one is reacting hyper-selectively. Another (concrete) situation would mean another type of behaviour, irrespective of similarities to previous experiences. Here are two examples:

> During a funeral everybody was weeping except one man. When asked why he wasn't weeping, he replied: 'I am not of this parish.' (Another church, another reaction.)

> Leslie, a girl with autism, kept up an unchecked stream of conversation in class – questions, answers, remarks. She kept on doing this, clearly unaware when this was appropriate and when not. She just blabbed away, saying what she felt like saying without restraint. Leslie's teacher found a solution. She would put the rules about talking in class in a visible form. She took a Polaroid photo of Leslie with her hand raised and placed it on the girl's desk, with the necessary explanation. This would make

everything clear: first you raise your hand, then you talk. It worked out perfectly. Leslie looked at the photo on her desk and then raised her hand, before speaking. The teacher was happy because the idea worked.

You can imagine her disappointment the following day when Leslie reverted to her old habits once again. The photo was still there? Yes. Then how could this be? After a while it became clear. The previous day, when Leslie had received the photo, she had been wearing a green sweater. The next day she was wearing red. Leslie interpreted the social rule quite literally on the detail level: she thought the rule applied only when she was wearing a green sweater, a 'green sweater situation'.

Another outer appearance, or detail, another form of behaviour. This is the way it works with individuals who have autism. They interpret social rules in terms of detail.

On the occasion of his sixth birthday, Johnnie is getting to wear his first long pair of trousers. He stands admiring himself in the mirror and asks:

'Tell me, Mummy, may I call you Cecilia now, just like Daddy?'

Life as a dotted line

Another pair of trousers, another rule. Another sweater, another rule.

It seems that Leslie with a green sweater experiences herself as a different person from the Leslie who wears a red sweater. Whenever an external detail changes, a person without a sense of coherence experiences a total change in the world around. There is no longer a unity, not one single world, but rather a multiplicity: many different situations. Thus neither an 'I-unity', but a multiplicity of 'I's. The person whose thinking is geared towards external details without cohesion has problems with the notion of *identity*.

This is the experience of a person with autism: another appearance, another person.

> On the eve of a war, a man arrives at an inn very late in the evening. Because of lack of space he has to share a room with a German officer. As he does not wish to meet this man, he asks the innkeeper to wake him very early in the morning. The man undresses and goes to sleep. When it is still dark outside, he is awakened by the innkeeper. The man quickly dresses and steps outside. To his amazement, a group of German soldiers are standing there. Not only that, they are saluting him. When, later, he gets on the train and passes a mirror, he notices he is wearing a German uniform. 'What a stupid innkeeper,' the man shouts. 'He woke the wrong man!'[3]

You develop an identity by experiencing yourself as a unity, isolated from external details. You experience your own personality as a guiding thread throughout your own history. It is like a movie with you in the main role. For people without integrating intelligence, like the man who stayed at the inn, this is not the case. They experience life much less as a coherent whole with themselves as the driving force.

People with autism often have an exceptional memory for objective facts. In contrast, their retentive capabilities for the personal in events is fairly weak. When you ask a person with autism how the trip went, you might get something like this in explanation: We left at eight-thirty from Birmingham on the Intercity train to London. It was a type C–850 with eight carriages. We had seats in the fourth car. We stopped at Birmingham International, Coventry, Milton Keynes, Watford and Euston. We got off there and took the Number 73 bus... (This may continue for some time in the same vein.)

Very seldom will you receive a personal account. Individuals with autism store a collage of different images inside their memory. They register the events as a sequence of separate happenings but experience very little unity and coherence to their own person. It is as if they don't realise that they themselves have been part of the experience.[4] They register facts, names, dates, locations, but all of that without any attachment to their own selves.

> During one of the conferences by the Flemish Autistic Association, a young man was asked to tell his 'life story'.[5] What the boy Martin had to tell was not so much a story as a summary of facts, happenings, names, and dates. This is an example: 'School in Maria's Garden lasted for five years: 1972–1977. In Maria's Garden there were five pavilions and one Catholic chapel. I spent my first time in Maria's Garden in Pavilion 3, which is also the place where Father de Bie had his office. He also preached in the Catholic church. I spent only about one year in Pavilion 3 and then I went into the first grade (1972). In the evening there were also festivities in Pavilion 3, in 1972 on 19 March [his birthday][6] with seven candles on the birthday cake and I was allowed to go home every weekend', instead of once in three weeks.

Individuals with autism do not live in the setting of a novel but rather in a 'factual' logbook. Facts dominate their experiences.

> Helen, a girl with autism, continuously points out mistakes made by another student in her class. The teacher wants to show her that she is not always right and that the boy can do certain things of which Helen is not capable.
>
> The teacher: 'Helen, you learned something last week from John.'
>
> Helen: 'It wasn't last week; it was this week.'

Judgement of human nature by individuals with autism is more encyclopaedic than romantic. That does not relate only to their own selves but also to their understanding of others.

> When a young boy with autism mentioned that he was about to take a group trip to Cyprus, he was asked: 'A group trip? That

sounds great. And have you already met the other people in the group?'

His answer: 'Yes; I know what car they are driving.'

People with autism register facts in life; they do not process them into a coherent and meaningful interpretation.

Identity could also be called 'personal central coherence' – experiencing your own self as the cause of the cohesion in your own set of happenings.

Seen in this light, individuals with autism possess less personality than people without autism.[7] Self-consciousness lies at the basis of our 'being in the world'. We've become aware of this ever since the times of Descartes. *I think, therefore I am.* Being conscious of yourself as part of a much larger cohesion creates personality. It is this personality that allows us in turn to experience coherence in the social world. By experiencing yourself as a person, you manage to bring order in the confusion of ever-changing social situations operating by their own invisible rules. If, however, you experience social situations as isolated pictures, you are at the mercy of a chaotic and fragmented world. You are left with a disjointed 'I',[8] and then you ask, just like that child with autism: 'Mama, can you put me together, please, because I broke.'

People with autism live in the here and now more than we do. Lacking an imagination for personal experiences means that they have problems looking back on their own role in events. They don't experience themselves enough as star players in their own past. But they also experience difficulties with the future. They do not look far enough ahead and their behaviour is not tuned to future thought. This has consequences for anyone wanting to educate a person with autism. People with autism learn too little from their experiences. Experiences do not teach them lessons for the future. For that reason they will, more than other people, repeatedly stumble over the same stone.

The life of individuals with autism lacks *continuity*. There is no story line in their lives where one scene flows into the next, no continuing coherent thread. There is rather a dotted line where every dot represents a fact, unconnected to another. A past event is thus simply a past event. What's gone is gone.

An example of this is the case of Gunilla, a Swedish woman with autism. When her parents went on an Easter holiday and she went to stay with her grandparents, she thought she was going to a new father and mother. When her parents after their holidays came to pick Gunilla up at her grandparents, she was under the impression that they were her new parents. She noted the striking resemblance with her 'former' parents but did not understand that she was dealing with the same people. Every phase (parents, grandparents, the 'new' parents) formed a new, separate stage in her life. There was no continuing line... Every situation was new and unique and had no connection with the past.[9]

Copy-catting

In contrast with what is sometimes claimed, people with autism do want to participate in the social world. Many have a clear social interest and do their utmost to get a hold on that difficult social world. To that end, they develop survival strategies.

One of the ways in which they try to adapt themselves to social life is by aping or 'copy-catting' the behaviour of other people. If you don't quite know how to behave but you want to be social, then you copy others. People without autism use the same social survival strategy when they land in a situation where they are unfamiliar with cultural and social customs and habits, like being in a foreign country. They often remark: 'Let's watch how the others do it and then we'll do the same.' The more foreign the culture, the more autistic-like the behaviour of the visitors, even though they may not have autism.

The same kind of copy-catting is noticeable in people that find themselves immersed in an event in a totally different social class to the one in which they operate.

> Shortly after his election, the American President Calvin Coolidge invited a group of friends from the country to a dinner at the White House. Since in that overwhelming environment they felt somewhat intimidated and were afraid of making some social gaffes, they aped Coolidge in everything he did. When the President poured some coffee from his cup in his saucer, they did likewise. He added some cream and sugar; they did the same. Coolidge then placed the saucer down for his cat...[10]

The country folk mimicked everything without understanding the purpose of their actions. The purpose of behaviour points to the invisible relationship of that behaviour with a purpose attached to it: I may raise my hand to greet somebody, to make somebody come to a stop or to put a question to somebody. If you fail to grasp the reason for my raised hand, thus fail to understand the 'why', but you do observe that I engage in some kind of interaction with others, something which you would also like to achieve, then chances are that you will imitate my behaviour quite literally. This literal copy-catting, without an understanding of the 'why', happens frequently with individuals with autism.[11] They copy but they don't know what it is they are copying.

> Joey, a young man with autism, had been taught that one can make the acquaintance of a new person by asking certain questions. He had already observed many conversations and listened to questions. And thus he imitated. Every time Joey met somebody he questioned the person:
>
> 'What's your name?'
>
> 'Do you smoke?'
>
> 'You must know that smoking is not healthy?' (He asked this of non-smokers as well.)

'Do you drive a car?'

'What model?' (He was very interested in cars and auto mechanics.)

'Do you have a girlfriend?'

'Have you had sex?' (An adolescent, he had developed an interest in girls and the subject fascinated him.)

Joey always asked the same questions, since to adapt the questions to the context was beyond him. He copied a social formula without understanding the essence of it.

Hello, how are you?

What Joey did is a direct example of another social survival strategy used by individuals with autism: repetitive behaviour. They can learn routines, or they may develop them themselves. They frequently repeat a routine that they have previously used with success in similar situations. Falling back on successful routines is not a bad strategy, and all people use it. But because most of us have a grasp of context beyond just the literal behaviour, we manage to manipulate routines in many ways and apply the right one at the right moment. We repeat routines in the right context and adapt ourselves to circumstances. Literal repetition makes sense only in cases where the context happens to be the same. Once the context differs, mechanical repetition makes little sense.

In the course of a recruitment examination at the Gendarmerie, two applicants are nervously awaiting the last test: a session with the force's commander. The first applicant entered the office.

Commander: 'I shall put just one question to you. If you answer correctly, you pass. What is made of leather and worn on our feet?'

Applicant 1 frowns, sighs, scratches his head, thinks long and intently.

'Not so easy, Commander… May I ask a question?'

Commander: 'OK, but only one and then I want to hear your answer.'

Applicant 1: 'Are there laces in it?'

Commander: 'Yes.'

Applicant 1 thinks again, scratches his head but eventually finds the answer and says with great relief: 'Shoes!'

He is congratulated by the Commander and ushered out of the office where he tells the whole story to Applicant 2, trying to put him at ease. 'I was allowed one question. I asked him if there were laces in it and when he said 'yes', I knew.'

The second applicant in turn enters the office.

Commander: 'It is hanging on the wall and it tells you the time. What is it?'

Applicant 2 sighs, scratches his head, thinks long and strenuously. 'Not so easy, Commander. May I ask a question?'

Commander: 'OK, but only one and then I want to hear your answer.'

Applicant 2: 'Are there laces in it?'

Commander: 'Of course not!'

Applicant 2: 'In that case it's easy. Slippers.'

At a building camp in the secretariat of the Flemish Autistic Association, foreign students were lending a helping hand. One young man with autism who was visiting on and off was delighted at meeting all that exotic company. During his first visit he had noticed that his knowledge of English had been a great help in socialising. Students had talked to him and here and there he had been able to engage in a real conversation. Speaking English was successful social behaviour in that situation. Only…on his next visit he started addressing everybody in English, throwing around his 'Hello, how are you?' left, right, and centre, disregarding the fact that the building camp was finished and the foreign students had left for home long ago.

May I calculate you?

Because people with autism do not *feel* coherence, some of them are trying to calculate it. This is like computers, which do not feel what the result of a certain process is either. Computers do not think (in a Cartesian sense), they calculate. There exist, it is true, some 'smart' computers that can 'learn' from their experiences. Every time they are confronted by a problem, they register all data for that problem and the attendant successful solution, provided they have found it. In the case of new problems, they look on their hard drive for similarities with previous problems. If they find the same problem, they carry out the calculations they used in the past. This method of problem solving requires a lot of time: the registered facts need to be compared one by one with the current problem. The computer does not select the most obvious comparisons in advance, simply because it does not have a feel for the problems. It is exactly for that reason that even very smart computers take a lot more time than the human brain. The human brain will often get the connection in 'the blink of an eye'.

People with autism have quite a lot of difficulty in trying to grasp social situations in one glance. In such cases they, like computers, resort to comparing and calculating.

Roy, a young man with autism, is on a social skills training course.[12] Part of the training is aimed at teaching him to recognise and deal with emotions. Roy learns to recognise anger in his mother but he keeps having trouble with emotions. He does not grasp that people will not always act identically in the same situation: on one occasion his mother is angry when he breaks something, on another she is not. The degree of difference between emotions is also a stumbling block. Numerous gradations exist between being a little angry and being furious. Or the differences are often subtle and, even more problematic, unnoticeable. You cannot always see the difference between a little angry and angry. This distinction needs to be felt from context. To give the gradations in feelings a concrete form, Roy's teacher devised an aid for him: a ruler with gradations from 1 to 100. One is a normal feeling; 100 means furious. Now, Roy asks his parents when they are angry: 'Are you 30 or 50 angry?' He does not feel situations and the attendant emotions and needs to calculate them using his ruler. People with autism literally need to 'decipher' social situations.

Temple Grandin[13] mentions that she stores all sorts of situations in her head as videotapes. Whenever she comes across a situation where she no longer knows how to behave, she goes in search inside her head for the videotape with the situation that most resembles the one in which she finds herself.[14] She tries to find in her video collection an analogue to a social situation, in the same way that we, when we are at a loss for a word, have recourse to the dictionary.

All of this does, however, take a lot of time. Thus, people with autism often react slowly and display delayed reactions. Our world moves too fast for them and, frequently, we don't give them enough time to decipher it.

There exist no social signposts

Because people with autism only infrequently experience their own selves as whole integrated units, they experience problems in learning to understand others as units as well. Outward appearances are not so difficult to interpret. General behaviour, individual facial expressions, can be interpreted quite effortlessly by some individuals with autism. But the invisible relationship between the outward and the inward is often a riddle for them. It is the inward element in people (their feelings, ideas, wishes, desires…) that makes the outward (what they say and do) comprehensible. Just as the true meaning of a glass of water becomes clear only through the invisible relationships that are attached to it (Whose is it? For whom is it intended?), someone's behaviour takes on sense and meaning only when the connection is seen with the invisible inward element: the person's purpose. If you fail to grasp the purpose, you miss the whole point.

A couple in love, together on a park bench.

She: Are we getting married?

He: Who would care to have us?

A Belgian industrialist, a multi-millionaire, was asked by Belgian television to participate in a talk show. After giving all the details of the programme, the Belgian television representative asked: 'What do you think? Would a 5000 franc fee be satisfactory?'

'Yes, of course,' the industrialist says. 'One moment, please, I'll get my chequebook.'

A father is out shopping with his son, who has autism. They stop at a flower shop.

Father: Shall we buy some flowers?

Tom: Why?

Father: Well, we have been married for 15 years.

Tom: And to whom are you giving the flowers?

In order to understand someone's behaviour, you have to put yourself in his shoes. We put ourselves in someone else's shoes because we are aware that that person, like ourselves, possesses his own inner side, an inner world of ideas and feelings. This understanding has come to us spontaneously. There is a professional term for it: 'theory of mind'.[15] People with autism have difficulty developing that faculty. 'This implicit knowledge that every normal human being gathers and develops in the course of a lifetime, on the basis of experiences and intercourse with others, seems to be largely absent with Temple. For the lack of this knowledge she is forced to "calculate" the purpose and the mood sets of others, to try to make explicit by algorithms what for the rest of us is second nature.'[16]

Because people with autism have only limited ability for sensing the cohesion in social situations, they experience difficulties in their association with others. It is primarily the invisible rules and aspects of human interaction that present them with such problems.

Take emotions, for example. Individuals with autism are capable of naming emotions: 'Papa is angry', 'that lady is sad', 'my brother is happy'. To give outward signs of emotions a significance (i.e. recognising the feeling they imply) is not impossible for them, as this remains on the one-to-one relationship level. But to understand where the feeling originates is much more difficult.

Naming emotions and comprehending them are not of the same order.[17] In order to comprehend emotions one has to have a feel for the context. Tears are tears, they all look alike. But tears of sadness are different from tears of happiness, and we all shed tears when peeling onions. Even where you do see the difference between those three kinds of tears, sadness is not always the same sadness. To understand why a person is sad demands a great feel for context. It requires us to place things in their proper perspective. Outward, concrete and visible details do not suffice for understanding things in their perspective. If you wish to know someone else's perspective (what she sees, feels, or thinks), you need, as it were, to put yourself in her place, to crawl into her skin (or invade her mind), and from that vantage point look at the outside world. For the world itself and the things in it will not tell you how somebody else looks at the outside and experiences its aspects.

Two men find a mirror in the woods. One of them looks into it and says: 'Hey, I know this guy!'

The other says: 'Show me.' He grabs the mirror and exclaims: 'Of course, that's me.'

At the start of a training week for adolescents with autism, a game of making acquaintance was organised. Every participant was required to provide on a sheet of paper certain data about himself – appearance, hobbies, age, address – but not his name. They could provide these data by answering certain questions. The first question, for instance, was: 'How would you recognise me?' All sheets were shuffled and gathered together. Then, every participant in turn had to pick out one sheet and on the basis of the information guess the identity of the person who had filled it out. To the first question 'How would you recognise me?' two participants, Steven being one of them, had given the answer '*By my face*'.

A technically correct answer but not quite successful in terms of perspective. When Steven's sheet was picked, the poor soul whose turn it was had but little concrete information to go on. When he picked the wrong name, Steven called out aloud: 'Wrong!' That he had given the game away by doing that did not immediately occur to him. Fully convinced and proudly he added: 'Well, it's true, isn't it? You can recognise me by my face.'

In contrast to the regulations and signals of motorised traffic (cars etc.), most rules of interactive traffic are invisible. Social traffic does not rely on changing lights, or painted lines which visibly demonstrate how we should behave. This is true, for example, of the social rule of reciprocity. To use a different metaphor, social behaviour is a sort of table-tennis game and under the rule of reciprocity each player takes turns hitting the ball. Comprehension of this reciprocity presents persons with autism with a tall order. Contact with individuals with autism is often a one-way street; either it's your turn, or it's theirs.

Even when they try to discover via calculations why people behave the way they do, individuals with autism keep looking at things from a distance, often with great interest, even more frequently with great surprise. Like a scientist coming in contact with a strange culture. Or, in the words of Temple Grandin 'like an anthropologist on Mars'.

Notes

1.   This is particularly true for the large group of people with autism and those who are intellectually challenged. People with autism and of normal or high intelligence know (have learned?) that invisible relationships exist. Their problem, however, is that they see all possible relationships and do not make a sensible pre-selection of those that within the context are the most obvious and thus logical. Gifted people with autism are therefore rather blinded by relationships. They see too much.

2.   Lansdown in Jolliffe, Lansdown and Robinson (1992, p.16).

3.   From Blundell (1983).

4.   See the notes 'personal episodic memory' and 'sense of self' in Jordan and Powell (1995, pp.95–96).

5.   Conference 'Autisme: Voorbereiden op volwassenheid' ('Autism: Preparing for adulthood'), held on 16 May 1987. Proceedings published by the Vlaamse Vereniging Autisme.

6.   Martin is talking about 'his' own birthday. It should be noted that at the very beginning of the story he had made it clear that his birthday is 19 March.

7.   This does not imply that a person with autism is *less* of a person than other people. Persons with autism are unique individuals with their own characters, their own temperaments. By personality I mean the capacity to experience a personal unity. People with autism are in no way inferior (see also the last chapter).

8.   Autism has been and is still sometimes confused with schizophrenia. Schizophrenia is a personality disorder. Literally, the word schizophrenia means 'split personality'. Autism and schizophrenia share some clinical features, such as poverty of speech and an inability to initiate or sustain goal-directed activities. Both disorders share a similar disorganisation in speech and behaviour and problems with the integration and the unity of the individual's personality. The confusion between au-

tism and schizophrenia is accidental: in both cases there is a lack of unity, a lack of coherent identity. The current *Journal of Autism and Developmental Disorders* was previously titled the *Journal of Autism and Childhood Schizophrenia.*

Although there are some similarities, schizophrenia can be differentiated from autism, because of the later onset of the symptoms, the presence of true hallucinations and delusions and the duration of the psychotic symptoms (Szatmari 1998). In some cases, a person can have both disorders: it is possible for people with autism with normal abilities to develop schizophrenia during or after adolescence, especially if there has been a lack of adapted care and guidance.

9.   Gerland (1996, p.47). (Translation into English in 1997.)

10.   From Blundell (1983) (This story appears on p.21 in the Dutch translation.)

11.   Not only on the social level. This meaningless copy-catting happens also in language usage by people with autism. There is even a name for it: 'echolalia'. (See also Peeters and Gillberg (1998). The literal imitation of social behaviour is called 'echopraxy'.

12.   We 'picked' this very revealing example from Mulders, Hansen and Roosen (1996, p.139).

13.   In Sacks (1995) (p.311–312 in the Dutch translation).

14.   This calling up of video images in the mind is excellently portrayed in the movie *Being There*. This film, a forerunner of *Rain Man*, deals with a simple gardener (with autism?) who gets to advise the President of the USA. For years he has lived isolated from the outside world and is suddenly forced to face reality. His only referential holdfast for his behaviour is TV, which for all those years he has faithfully watched. The book is based on the novel by Jerzy Kosinski (1971) of the same title.

15.   There is an extensive body of literature on the notion of 'theory of mind' in autism. For a recent review on this topic, we refer to Baron-Cohen, Tager-Flusberg and Cohen (2000). In this book the reader will find a chapter where Francesca Happé reviews research on 'weak central coherence' and its relation to deficits in theory of mind: Happé (2000).

16.   Sacks (1995) p.299 in the Dutch translation.

17.   See Vermeulen (1997, p.78).

CHAPTER 5

The Button Man
About communication

Symbols create a shared world

Communication is the prime medium for imbuing things with significance. It represents the inter-human traffic of meanings. Via communication, meaning is transferred from one person to another.

When I am thirsty and I want the waiter to bring me a glass of water, I need to communicate my wish. It is not possible for the waiter to actually *observe* my thirst or my intention of ordering something to quench it. Feelings, wishes and ideas have significance only within me and thus are not noticeable to outsiders. I am thirsty and I imagine a glass of water. I imagine a waiter bringing me a glass of water. In Figure 5.1 you can *observe* me thinking about a waiter bringing me a glass of water.

Figure 5.1

But do you actually see the glass of water? Can you see the waiter? No, for both are present only within me.

In one way or another I need to express my wish and make it known to the waiter. I need to give form to it.

I opt for the following form:

Figure 5.2

Now my thirst and my wish to order something have become noticeable. I have 'expressed' what was inside me, brought it out into the open, given it form. The waiter observes my wish and in turn assimilates within himself my expression for a glass of water: he assigns meaning to it. He processes the observed information (I understand the gentleman wants a glass of water) and he brings me what I ordered.

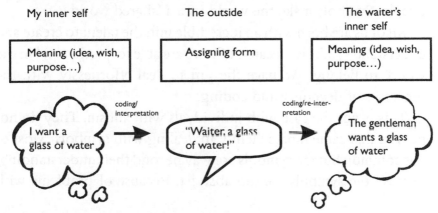

Figure 5.3 Communication as a process of coding and decoding

This is communication, a very simple process. It is merely a question of 'coding' and 'decoding', of interpreting and re-interpreting.

Communication is assigning form and unravelling form. The form is called 'language'. Language is the means by which we communicate meaning to others and receive signals with meaning in return. Language is the instrument for assigning form to meaning.

Meanings can receive form in different ways. When you want to order water, you have different forms of language at your disposal, and can dress up ideas in different ways:

- *Spoken language* ('water, de l'eau, agua, vatten...'). In our world, spoken language is the most commonly used form of assigning form to things. It is also the easiest. We carry this instrument with us at all times: our own body, more specifically our vocal cords, our mouth, tongue...

- *Written language* (water, vatten, aqua...)

- *Symbolic language* (drawings and photos)

- *Body language* (gestures – the gesture used for drinking)

- *Object language* (you raise an empty glass to the waiter).

All these different forms of 'language' are references. They point to underlying, invisible meanings. References are identical to symbols. Language is thus a system composed of symbols. Without symbols there can be no communication, no interaction amongst people. Symbols make the world into a 'shared world'.

All of us are born with an incredible gift: the talent to create and understand symbols. Because of it we are able to 'participate' in the world, to belong. We have the gift to deal effortlessly with the processes of decoding and coding.

This is not the case with individuals with autism. They do not possess that same innate facility in dealing with symbols. Most of our common human symbols are way beyond their understanding, because the symbols are too abstract. Because of problems with their imaginative faculties, individuals with autism get regularly bogged down in the (de)coding processes.[1]

Interpretation errors

In addition to problems with imagination and abstractions individuals with autism experience particular problems with the coherence between inter-related symbols and their connection with a given context.[2] This coherence, as in the case of social behaviour, is not objectively observable. For people who don't have autism, that is people capable of coherent thought, this is not really a problem since coherence is evident, it need not be emphasised. The communication happens automatically. However, for people who cannot so quickly grasp the whole picture, coding and decoding, interpreting and re-interpreting is a difficult task. Not surprisingly, computers and individuals with autism tend to make a lot of mistakes in their interpretation (translation) of things. Their interpretations are indeed very literal ones.

Literal translations are done on the basis of one-to-one relationships: one symbol has one meaning. In literal translations, symbols are treated as isolated details, without thought for their mutual coherence. We can compare this with the way one learns a new language – Spanish for instance. You begin by learning the meaning of separate words.

glass	=	vaso
waiter	=	camarero
water	=	agua
to bring	=	llevar
to be able	=	poder
you	=	usted
my	=	me
a	=	un
of	=	de

A computer also uses 'symbols' in this way: one key = one function or meaning:

F1	=	print
F2	=	copy
F3	=	close

So far this is simple. It becomes difficult when the details are combined into a coherent whole, such as in the sentence: 'Waiter, can you bring me a glass of water?' If you are translating only on the level of detail, that is 'word for word', you get no further than:

Waiter	can	you	bring	me	a	glass	of	water
⇩	⇩	⇩	⇩	⇩	⇩	⇩	⇩	⇩
Camarero	poder	Usted	llevar	me	un	vaso	de	agua

Figure 5.4

At first sight this seems OK. An accommodating Spanish waiter will understand what you want and bring you a glass of water. But he will find it humorous, for it is hardly fluent Spanish.

The right way is: 'Camarero, podria traerme un vaso de agua?' Quite a difference, isn't there?

To move from the level of loose words to that of sentences is not so simple. It is no longer a question of knowing the words. Now you have to consider the appropriate grammatical rules, declensions, conjugations, prepositions, adverbs etc. In your own experience, you have probably had some tough times trying to master foreign languages. You understand the difficulties. To make up sentences or to understand sentences is an art. It surely should not surprise you that some individuals with autism communicate only by means of isolated words and not in the more natural flowing language of grammatical constructions. In their eyes, we are 'magicians' with words.

The most common word-processing programs function on the level of isolated words. Most spelling control programs check for misspelled words but do not detect grammatical errors or nonsensical meanings (although there are some, more complex programs that do to an extent). To the standard home PC, the following nonsense word combination seems perfectly correct since, on the level of isolated words, everything is quite OK: 'The woman yesterday will his egg run out meter by meter of buses horses weave.' In the same way, people with autism do not quickly identify nonsensical language constructions.

Some kids with autism are being taught about 'double' and 'half'. The teacher asks Richard to read a sentence from the workbook: 'double in the opposite of half'. Richard reads what is written. He doesn't notice anything wrong. But we have immediately noticed the spelling mistake in the sentence: 'in' needs to be changed to 'is'. The teacher asks Richard to read the sentence a second time. When she asks him if the sentence is correct, he gets confused. He doesn't understand. The other children in the class do not react. None of the four children present notices the mistake. All words, individually taken, are correct. The word 'in' is a proper word, yet, when taken in context, it is wrong. Sentences are more than just a compilation of loose words. The whole is more than the sum of the isolated parts. But this is not so for people with autism, and neither is it for computers.

Tshe parents can now summer back on

Once I wrote a report on a boy called Jan. When I was asked to make a similar report about Lynn I went over the previous report using my computer. Why rewrite everything when the computer offers so many possibilities? Why reinvent the wheel? My word processor includes a very interesting function: replace. By using the mouse and the keys I can have one word in a document changed into another word. So I started. The previous report dealt with a boy, this one with a girl. I had the computer change the name 'Jan' to 'Lynn' but also changed the personal pronouns 'him' → 'her', 'his' → 'her', 'he' → 'she'. Since Lynn was seen by me in the summer and the report on Jan was made in the fall, I also gave the computer the command to change 'fall' into 'summer'.

The end result was astonishing. After the computer had changed all of the passages, I was presented with the following:

> Lynn was referred to us at tshe end of Lynnuary for a revaluation of her functional skills. In tshe summer wshen we did an assessment her self-care skills, Lynn displayed more of an interest than last time. Her test results are thus better than tshe on tshe previous occasion. She was particularly interested in sorting out laundry, especially shirts. As it appears, she does ther also at home. Her parents are pleased with ther. Tshe parents can now summer back on the domestic skills Lynn has acquired to keep her busy during long periods of free time.

The computer had processed two kinds of incorrect substitutes, and one was my own fault. I had neglected to click on the command to replace only 'complete words'. Because of this failure, the computer searched for literal combinations of the details that I entered, whether they were complete words or not.[3] Thus 'January' beacame 'Lynnuary', 'the' was changed to 'tshe' and 'this' to 'ther'. In a clear case of over-generalisation, the computer had changed too many things, including words I did not want it to change. I had failed to make my instructions sufficiently detailed and formal. Computers and people with autism need specific instructions.

My computer also made another mistake, and this one had nothing to do with unclear or vague instructions; it rather pertained to an absence of coherence.

Many words do not always have the same function in sentences. They may have different meanings, sometimes as adjectives, sometimes adverbs, sometimes pronominal. The rules of grammar are not static but flexible. In order to find out the meaning of words in the context of the sentence, you have to take into account their total coherence as it relates to context, the relation to other words in the sentence. But this kind of relationship is too difficult for my computer. This is the reason why it changed 'fall back on' to 'summer back on'.

I once had lunch with a young man with autism. When we were finished, the telephone rang. I asked him to clean up in the meantime. After the one telephone call came another, and still another. Many telephone calls and some time later I noticed that the man was still busy in the kitchen. I went to take a look. He was busy cleaning out cupboards. My instructions had not been sufficiently detailed and precise. I had meant him to clear the table and to do the dishes...but I had failed to be specific (literal) enough.

People with autism tend to misinterpret things a lot, simply because they do not grasp the coherence of one word with other words in the sentence. Just like us, when we start learning a new language, and just like the computer, they make fixed and separate associations of words and meanings. That a word could have various meanings and that a meaning could possibly change with the context is 'incomprehensible' to them.

> Every time Bart goes to the sea, his parents tell him 'we're off to the beach, Bart'. Bart understands this quite well. One fine Sunday evening, Bart's parents take him to visit some relations. The highways are clogged as many people are returning from their weekend outings to the sea. Bart's mother says to his father: 'I guess it was busy at the beach.' This remark panics Bart. He becomes totally confused. He hears the word 'beach' but their car is not going in the direction of the beach. (Bart knows the way. As a processor of 'details' he obtains his information from noticeable details.) 'Beach' means to him 'going to the beach'.

The word 'beach' within a sentence can have a number of different meanings. Everything depends on its connection with the other words in the sentence. Prepositions, in particular, those innocuous words that by themselves have no meaning, can change the meaning of the whole: e.g. to the beach, at the beach, on the beach, near the beach…

For a lot of people with autism, concentrating as they do on concrete, visible details, these differences are too abstract. Prepositions are only vague, nonsensical sounds. Have you ever undergone the preposition 'in' as a 'live' experience? A car happens to be more concrete. You can see it, touch it, sit in it. That provides much stronger information for the person with autism, and it is much more meaningful than the nonsensical sounds of prepositions.

Try to picture yourself in the concrete thought-world of a person with autism. Bart has on many occasions experienced the sound 'beach' as he is being taken somewhere in the car. And every time in the past, his family took him to the beach. Bart's brain fashions the following association in terms of meaning:

Sitting in the car   +   hearing the word 'beach'   =   to go to the beach

Bart is sitting in the car and hears the word 'beach' yet they are taking another direction. A bit confusing, isn't it?

Anyone who, like Bart, lives in a world of isolated associations and connects words to concrete, observable experiences instead of seeing their coherence with other words, is bound to be confronted with some unpleasant surprises – because car + beach does not always mean 'to go to the beach'.

But it is not only people with autism who may be in for a surprise in these situations. Many children with autism are thought to comprehend the spoken language. And, yet, they react often in strange ways.

Steven is playing in the living room. His mother has prepared dinner and calls out from the kitchen 'Steven, everything's ready.' Steven takes his seat at the table. That's the way it always is. Steven appears to understand what his mother says. One day, his mother calls out: 'Steven, please open the door.' Somebody has rung the doorbell and Mother is busy making mayonnaise. But Steven goes and takes his accustomed place at the table.

Steven is not reacting just to the words but to other information. What has Steven learned?

Smells the food and sees that the table is set	+	hears mother say something	=	sit at the table

Steven has learned that something is expected from him when he hears his name called. And when he hears his name called and sees the table set for dinner and smells the food, that means he is to go to the table for dinner. Vision and smell give more concrete clues than his mother's words.

The button man

There are, however, people with autism who do comprehend and use sentences. Some of them can read and write. In contrast to Bart and Steven, for whom words are only loose details, they are able to co-ordinate words. The coherence between the words represents no problem, as the cohesion between them is explicit. It is expressed, and the differences between words are obvious and comprehensible: 'to the beach' and 'from the beach' sound different; they thus signify different meanings.

Nonetheless, even these persons with autism have difficulties with language. The significance of quite a number of words is not only dependent on the externally observable cohesion with other words in the sentence but also – and particularly – on the invisible cohesion with the context.[4]

> During a gala dinner in a foreign country, a highly placed official needs to go to the toilet. As he doesn't know where the toilet is, he whispers very discreetly into his neighbour's ear: 'The toilet?'
>
> The neighbour: 'The other side.'
>
> As a result, the official gets up and whispers the question into his neighbour's other ear.

The 'I–You' confusion already remarked on by Leo Kanner in 1943 as characteristic of autism is a typical example of problems with the invisible coherence of words. The word 'I' can refer to anyone. When you are referring to your own self you use 'I', but when someone else talks about *himself* he will use the same pronoun. Since children with autism lay down fixed associations between outward things and words, and since they are always addressed with 'you', some think that they are 'you' and that 'you' always refers to their own selves. They attach their own image to the word 'you', calling themselves 'you' and another person 'I'. It is too difficult for certain persons with autism to understand that the 'I' image can change, namely with any other person who is talking about himself.

> She: Darling, if there were a fire, whom would you save first, yourself or me?
>
> He: Me.

The 'I–You' phenomenon might make it appear that individuals with autism exchange or reverse different people. This is not the case. They are not exchanging the 'I' and 'You' roles, they are just assigning a different meaning to them. They attach the personal pronouns to one defined person and fail to understand that the person to whom these words refer can change depending on the context in which the words are used.

Many words admit of multiple meanings; two or more. You will get to the true meaning only when you place the message in its proper context. The literal, concrete interpretation won't help you one bit, and neither will looking up the word in a dictionary.

Try to translate a Swedish text, using only a dictionary and a grammar book. It won't be very successful. A good translation is based on a total interpretation and understanding of the text. You need background information, that is you need to grasp the theme of the text to be translated. Experienced interpreters from the world of politics not infrequently miss the point when they are doing translations for conferences on autism.

Computers have a problem when they run into imagery in a sentence, or when the meaning of the word is dependent on the context of the sentence. Computers can perform impressive feats, but only when their commands are formal and fixed and invariable rules exist to guide them (such as in the case of calculations or chess problems).[5] Computers are rigid and literal translators. This is the reason why translation programs come up with so much nonsense:

Dutch: Mijn arm is lam (My arm is paralysed).

French computer translation program: Mon pauvre est agneau (my poor is lamb) – because 'arm' in Dutch means 'poor' as well as 'arm as a body part', and 'lam', in addition to its meaning 'paralysed', signifies the animal 'lamb'.

The same mistakes are also made by people who possess just a 'little knowledge' of a language. All too often they translate too literally because they lack the feel for the nuances that are characteristic of every language.

A foreign politician was giving a speech in French about his career. He started out as follows: 'Quand je regarde mon derrière, je le vois divisé en deux parties…'

What he wanted to say was: 'When I look behind me [into the past], I notice two things in my life…'

What he actually said was: 'When I look at my behind, I see it divided into two parts...'

The language doesn't even have to be foreign. Our own tongue is full of words for which the correct meaning can only be grasped within the context of their use.

Try to picture images to go with the following words: pigboat, butterball, wheelsucker, moonface, pub-crawler, hellcat, elbow room. These are existing words, all of them to be found in the dictionary.

And what kind of picture do you imagine for a button man?

Figure 5.5

This could well be the picture for a button man. At least, in the context of a fairy tale. But try to apply this picture in the following context.

After months of research and undercover work, the police finally arrested the man. He was brought to the police office and interrogated. When the officers discovered that the man was just a button man, they were very disappointed. He was not the big leader they thought him to be and as a button man, he could not give them much useful information about the organisation.

Do you perhaps get the feeling of ravioli in a doll's crib? Of a washbasin at a railway station ticket window?

A button man is a low-ranking member of an organised crime syndicate.

Words of double entendre and imagery are inexhaustible sources of jokes. Taking a language literally can lead to preposterous reactions and pronouncements:

> Doctor to a not-so-young patient: So then, sir, you are pushing eighty?
>
> Patient: Yes, but pulling too.

> 'What do you think of sex on TV?'
>
> 'Quite painful, thank you.'
>
> 'Painful?'
>
> 'Yes, I tried it once and I fell off.'

Many anecdotes about people with autism are based on literal interpretation of language.

> In a church, a mother sees the deacon approaching with the collection plate. She tells her daughter who has autism: 'You can throw your pennies in the basket.' The daughter gets up and with a mighty swing pitches her money towards the deacon.

> During gym class, the boys are asked to pull themselves up on the rack and swing back and forth. Nick has managed to pull himself up but is hanging immobile. The teacher says: 'Come on, Nick, you must start moving your arms!' Nick lets go, drops to the gym floor and starts waving his arms at the teacher, smiling broadly.

There is, however, a still greater difficulty for people with autism. And this is created by people who think in terms of integrated coherence.

What is left unsaid

People who do not have autism are used to dealing with people who, like themselves, can spontaneously and quickly grasp the context of what is being said. Everybody, indeed, possesses something like 'theory of mind', the notion that others think (differently). This makes the purpose of other people's behaviour clear, even though the purpose itself is invisible.

For people used to integrated coherent thinking, it is so self-evident that others extract information from associations that they tend to use words very economically. Their normal communications don't waste a lot of words. Take the following:

'Waiter, a glass of water!'

What does this expression mean? Not a very difficult question, you may say. Mistake! Read it again. It doesn't say what it means. In fact, it can mean many things, as demonstrated by the following examples. What is between brackets is left unsaid but may indicate the true meaning.

'Waiter, [look over there, it's] a glass of water!' (Meant as a remark.)

'[But] waiter, [that is] a glass of water!' ('I ordered a beer!' Meant as a remark but different from the previous one.)

'Waiter, [here you have] a glass of water!' (Meant as an offer.)

'Waiter, [would you like] a glass of water [?]!' (A question.)

'Waiter, [would you bring me] a glass of water?' (A different question.)

Which of the five possibilities contains the correct meaning of the expression will be made clear only if the sentence is placed into its proper context. This would encompass:

- the facial expression of the person (questioning, annoyed...)
- the accompanying gestures (pointing, both hands raised, one hand raised...)
- the circumstances (who is serving whom, is there an empty glass already...).

People who think using integrated coherence, people without autism, generally experience no trouble in finding the correct meaning or interpretation of pronouncements. The context tells them what is meant. But at this level of communication, all computers have to throw in the towel. For instance, it is not possible for a computer to find out the meaning of the word 'it' in the following sentence: 'The boys don't want an ice cream because it is too cold.'[6] Our integrating intelligence has no trouble with this sort of sentence. Spontaneously, our thoughts jump to 'it' as the weather. Because of the context (you are also experiencing the cold) it is self-evident that 'it' does not refer to the ice cream. Equally, for that matter, it is obvious that a moustache is not a sales product.

Wife: There is man at the door with a moustache.

Husband: Tell him I already have a moustache.

Imagine that computers could create pictures from sentences. What kind of picture would they generate from the sentence: 'I saw the dog with my binoculars'? The incorrect interpretation of the context can lead to humorous and absurd situations. Whenever the most obvious and expected interpretation 'between the lines' is replaced by one that is less obvious and totally unexpected...the result is absurdity. Below are some examples.

(Analysing jokes is a rather pointless exercise. It makes jokes lose their effect. Nonetheless, try in the following anecdotes to list the ambiguities which lead to misunderstanding. I have done it myself, but in order not to spoil the fun the analyses are added to the endnotes.)

Judge: Smith, you are here for lechery.

Smith: Fine by me. I'm ready for the ladies.[7]

After he has examined the patient, the doctor says: 'I cannot give a diagnosis with complete certainty. I think the problem is alcohol.'

The patient replies 'In that case, Doctor, why don't I come back when you're sober?'[8]

A man enters a store that sells flags. After he has browsed for a while, he is approached by a salesman who asks if he can be of assistance. 'I'm looking for a green Belgian flag,' the man says.

'Sorry, sir,' the salesman says, 'but the Belgian flag comes only in black, yellow, and red.'

After some thought, the customer says: 'All right then, give me a black one.'[9]

The lady of the house says to her maid: 'Annie, I have bought a toilet brush. Will you use it from now on?'

After a while, Annie comes back to the lady and says: 'Madam, I used the toilet brush. It is a bit rough. I prefer to use paper.'[10]

People with autism experience their greatest communication problem with what is *not* being said. What is not expressed remains invisible, not observable in concrete terms. Meaning is hidden within the context, which contains the information that is necessary to fully understand what is actually expressed. Because people with autism are slower in grasping context, they lack the information that is necessary to comprehend the whole. Often they react only to part of the whole. They react in a literal sense.

> Paul's grandma knows that her grandson with autism will be going on his first school trip in two weeks. She comes visiting and asks him: 'And when are you leaving on your school trip?' To which Paul replies: 'At a quarter past eight.'

> As part of their social skills training, young boys with autism were asked to write an essay about friendship. The title was: 'How to make friends'. Twelve-year-old Michael wrote: 'Atoms, cells, eyes, nose, mouth, arms, legs. P.S. Then say "hello".'[11]

Hidden purposes

What is left unsaid is often the *purpose* of the message. The purpose is not elicited from the words themselves but from the context.[12] Specialists in communication talk about the 'relational level' and the 'content level' of the communication. The content is the words. Why and for what purpose you use the words depends on the involvement or the relationship between you and the person to whom your message is directed.[13]

Usually we start from the premiss that the relationship between ourselves and the receiver of the message is sufficiently clear. For that reason, we do not elaborate on that relationship in the words we use. It would be too long-winded and laborious and sound rather strange. Imagine that you are a waiter and a customer who wants a glass of water addresses you in the following way: 'Waiter, a glass of water, please. Listen, what I mean is this. I'm sitting here and I am thirsty. I would love to have a glass of water to drink. And since you are the waiter, and I am addressing you, the idea expressed in the first sentence I directed to you is that you should bring me a glass of water, here to this table.'

Communication is a complex affair. You not only need to grasp the words by themselves and their inter-relationship (their meaning), but also to comprehend the social world that lies hidden behind the words: the purpose behind the words. Is 'Waiter, a glass!' a question? An order? An observation? Is your teacher correcting or giving information? Is the employee giving an answer or asking a question?

Child: Miss, I has slept with Daddy last night.

Teacher: No, it is, 'I have slept with Daddy last night.'

Child (surprised): But, Miss, I has not seen you there.

Customer: Miss, can you tell me how long the flight from Brussels to New York is?

Airline clerk: Just a moment, sir.

Customer: Thank you, miss.

People with autism all tend to commit the same mistakes in interpretation. Their inability to understand the coherence in communication (idea) is closely related to the problems they experience with social coherence (context). The social aspect of communication presents the greatest stumbling block for them. However gifted they may be, the idea behind the communication often escapes them. The most essential aspect of the communication (the idea) cannot be experienced in its literal sense. Ideas are seldom expressed literally, in fact, they are not expressed but rather left unsaid. For people with autism, the ideas behind the communication are, literally, a secret.

It is bitterly cold. Frank, a young man with autism, is on the point of leaving for work. The group leader tells him to take his cap and gloves. Frank nods and a little later leaves. The group leader looks out and sees him getting on his bike without cap or gloves. She calls out: 'Frank, I told you to take your cap and gloves.'

Frank turns to her and says: 'Yes, I have them with me.' He pulls them from his coat pocket as proof.

It is a known fact that children with autism often do not react to group instructions. The teacher in a kindergarten class tells the children 'take your book' and everybody does so, except the boy with autism. He does not quite understand that the command, the instruction, is meant for him as well. The teacher did not specifically mention his name.

The opposite too can happen.

A mother tells her son 'fetch your jacket'. The sister with autism leaves the room and gets her own jacket. She is not capable of deducing that her mother's instruction is meant for her brother, not for her.

As a result of this inability to grasp the 'unexpressed' idea behind the communication, people with autism often react only to what is explicitly stated and not to what is actually, but implicitly, meant. That too is a form of literal comprehension.

The teacher says, 'Ben, go to the toilet.' Ben runs to the toilet and remains standing there. He did not understand that he was supposed to actually 'use' the toilet; the teacher did not explicitly tell him so. As in the case of computers, you have to give people with autism precise instructions if you want to avoid their doing the wrong thing or doing something the wrong way.

The problems that people with autism experience with language do not concern only its spoken aspect, the words, the sentences. Other forms of communication also require a good sense of interpretation of the context, even for somebody with good comprehension. This is certainly true of gestures, facial expressions, body language, and other 'non-verbal' communication. Often, these forms are even more difficult for people with autism. The meaning of words can be looked up in dictionaries, but there exists no dictionary for gestures. Gestures are even less explicit or 'explanatory' than words. The gesture of pointing belongs to that category. You have to deduce from the context what the object of the gesture is. You have to be able to put yourself in the shoes of the person who is pointing in order to find out to what this person wants to draw your attention. You have to 'get inside' the ideas, wishes and feelings of other people. But this is not always so easy if you happen to be socially naïve, like a person with autism or somebody like Mr Bean.

> During the Christmas shopping rush, when everyone is buying gifts, Mr Bean is standing with his fiancée in front of a jeweller's window. In front of a publicity photo featuring a moonstruck couple lies a gorgeous diamond ring. Mr Bean's fiancée points to it and he smiles and nods his head understandingly. On Christmas Eve he hands her a package with his Christmas present. All excited, she opens it and finds the publicity photo.

Even though people with autism may know a host of words, the question of *how* you communicate your message – *why, for how long, when* – remains difficult for them. Recent studies have demonstrated that certain types of communication skills, that can be mastered by two-year-olds, remain insufficiently developed in individuals with autism. So, for instance, every form of communication that presupposes shared attention tends to go awry with people with autism. They fail to check whether others are paying enough attention to what they have to communicate.[14]

A major mystery for people with autism is finding the way to adapt their communication to other people, to the context. This is not to say they don't try. But just as in the case of social behaviour, their efforts don't often proceed past some ineffective copy-catting.

> A young man on vacation calls home and gets his brother, who has autism, on the line: 'How's our cat Oscar?'
>
> 'Oscar died this morning.'

'That's terrible! You know how I like him. Couldn't you have told me a little more carefully?'

'What do you mean?'

'Well, you could have said that he was sitting on the roof. Next time I called, you could say he was still sitting up there and nobody could get him down. You could have gradually prepared me for the bad news.'

'Yes, I get you. Sorry.'

'OK. How's Mum?'

'She's sitting on the roof.'[15]

Notes

1. I will not delve any deeper into the problems with abstract language in this book. Amongst others, Theo Peeters has described this topic extensively in his last two books: Peeters (1997) and Peeters and Gillberg (1998).

2. Here I am referring to the two 'higher' levels of language. The simplest level is the *semantic*: the connection between words and things (meanings). The two higher levels are the *syntactic*, the inter-relationship of words, the cohesion between meanings; and the *pragmatic*, the cohesion of words (series) within the context.
   People with autism have problems on all three levels but their problems increase as complexity on the various levels increases. They experience the most problems with the pragmatic aspects of communication.

3. Just as a sentence is more than the sum of its words, words are more than letters placed in a row. For a computer, which cannot deduce sense from context, words are nothing more than consecutive symbols. Thus, the word 'he' is no more than two letters 'H and E' placed beside each other. If we see (or hear) the word 'he', we think intuitively of something male, a man...

4. These words are known as 'referential words'. Referential words are words without a fixed meaning that borrow their meaning from the subject they refer to: for example, large (something is large in comparison with something else: a mouse is large when reference is made to a beetle but not large at all in comparison with an elephant), yesterday (this becomes today the day after and becomes tomorrow one day further on), above and below (the second storey is above the first but below the third). Studies show that people with autism experience great difficulties with referential words.

5. Paulos (1985).

6. This example, and the following one about the dog, is taken from Penzias (1990). (Both appear on p.58 in the Dutch translation.)

7.   The difference between 'for' in the sense of 'being convicted because of' and 'to be here to commit lechery'.

8.   'I think that (your) drinking problem is the cause' as opposed to 'I think that (my) drinking problem is the cause'.

9.   The flag is only available in a combination of three colours (black-yellow-red) versus a flag that comes in three individual colours (black, yellow and red).

10.   The brush is meant for cleaning the toilet as opposed to cleaning oneself.

11.   This anecdote is taken from Twachtman (1995, p.136).

12.   The grammar of a sentence, the phonetics, is also called the surface-structure of that sentence. The actual contextual significance of the sentence is the in-depth structure, which is not visible (Hofstadter 1979).

13.   It is not my intention to elaborate on this any further, though it is a very interesting topic. The level of relationship, for instance, is often given form via non-verbal communication. For people with autism, it is especially the incongruities between what is said and how it is said that are unfathomable. In terms of relational levels, people with autism are particularly inept and naïve.

14.   Phillips *et al.* (1995). When asking for help, children with autism use a strategy whereby the adult present is used as an observant subject much less frequently than other people.

15.   From Paulos (1985).

CHAPTER 6

Applefries
About rigidity

Aut(omat)ism

> 'My brothers thought the word "autistic" looked a bit like "automatic".'[1]

Humour results when people act a bit like automatons, when human behaviour is comparable to that of a machine, according to the philosopher Henri Bergson a century ago.

Machines are not flexible in the ways they operate. They carry out the jobs for which they were designed, nothing more, nothing less. Machines have no consciousness and are thus not capable of controlling or adapting their own 'behaviour'. Put a car in gear and off it goes. And it keeps on going, even though a tree or some other obstacle may suddenly appear in its path. Without a driver, the car is unable to adjust its 'behaviour' to the changed circumstance. It just runs straight into the tree.

Give a computer a command and it will carry it out. Tell it to print and it goes through the motions, even though the page may be blank and it makes no sense to print it. The computer does not see the pointlessness of the exercise and prints. It does not tell you that you would be better off just using the blank, unprinted page.

Whenever people begin to act like cars or computers and fail to adapt their behaviour to prevailing conditions, some funny situations may result. When somebody who is walking about and looking up at the stars suddenly stumbles over a stone, it creates a situation that makes us laugh. It is no longer so comical if we know that falling down was the person's conscious choice.

> When the globetrotter returned to his country after an absence of many years, he was seen to drop down on his knees and kiss the ground.
>
> 'An emotional experience, isn't it?' a reporter asked.
>
> 'It isn't that,' the globetrotter said. 'It's a banana peel.'

The one for Warrington stood at the very back…
About the essence of things

The ability to see cohesion, or being capable of central coherence, allows us the flexibility to adapt our behaviour to changing and changed situations. Coherent thinkers do not experience their life as a succession of isolated instances but as one continuing process. No sequence of isolated frames but one connected roll of film. They integrate every happening, every experience into the total picture. In this way, a rich and multi-faceted base of experience is being created which they can call upon in the future in order to understand new situations and to react to them meaningfully.

This is not the case with people who lack central coherence. Experiences are coupled to concrete situations. While the whole is not understood, the details are seen as connected to each other, and this connection is used as an absolute in future situations. Whenever the one happens, the other is bound to follow.

That details become very important is understandable if you don't take an overview of their cohesion. But if details become more important than the whole, the result is machine-like behaviour; rigid, inflexible. Flexibility presupposes sensitivity to context, an eye for the obstacle in the way, even while you are putting the car in gear. Sensitivity to context means having an understanding of the essence of a situation, being able to separate the important from the non-important. This ability stands in direct opposition to an orientation towards concrete details. Details are in fact often unimportant.

A platoon of soldiers is ordered to sabotage a train station. They return after a couple of hours.

Sergeant: Mission accomplished, sir.

Commander: But I didn't hear an explosion.

Sergeant: No, but we did something just as effective. We removed all the train tickets.

Two men from Warrington have gone on a binge in Liverpool and missed the last bus. They decide to 'borrow' one from the bus terminal. One keeps watch at the gate while the other enters the depot. It takes him a long time and his friend hears all sorts of horrible crashing noises issuing from inside. Finally, the man emerges with a badly dented bus. His companion asks: 'What the dickens was that all about?'

The other says: 'It wasn't so easy, you know. The one for Warrington stood at the very back…'

The person who is sensitive to context is also able to place every detail correctly within a given situation and to locate the multiple elements in their proper order and perspective. (The proper order and inter-connectivity create coherence.) Cohesive thinkers achieve this ordering spontaneously and according to a well-defined principle, the principle of importance. In order to sift out the important details from the unimportant ones, one must scrutinise the idea or the meaning of the situation. To 'get to the bottom of it' you need imagination, very frequently social imagination, since ideas are drawn by people and not by objects. Once the idea, the notion, has been made clear, certain details will become less important than others.

To make a train move, tickets are much less of a necessity than railway tracks or an engine. If you want to drive away, it's not important what the routing panel on the bus says, as long as the bus has an engine and moves.

> Peter has just got married and is looking urgently for a place to live. An estate agent informs him that there are no houses available on the market at that time.
>
> 'Come back in a year,' Peter is told.
>
> 'With pleasure,' Peter says. 'Should I come in the morning or in the afternoon?'

People with autism have difficulty placing things in perspective. They have too little insight in the idea of situations. They are less oriented towards the meaning of situations and concentrate far more on the literal observation of details. That is why all details receive the same value and are considered equally important.

This has a serious impact on behaviour. We have already described the consequences for social behaviour and communication. Yet the impact goes deeper. The learning and execution of nearly all behaviours or activities suffer under autistic hyper-selectivity and literal interpretation. People with autism are controlled in much of their behaviour by details, which results in a certain rigidity in their behavioural patterns. This sort of inflexibility has many names: rigidity, resistance to change, stereotyped behaviour, ritualistic behaviour. These are all different expressions of one and the same problem: the problem of flexible generalisation – either a lack of it or an excess.

- A lack of generalisation occurs when you do not apply a previously learned behaviour or activity in similar situations, when in your behaviour you are oriented towards one particular detail and you fail to react when that detail happens to be absent from the situation, even though the situation itself is 'identical' or essentially the same. You carry out a certain action only when the detail in question is present.

- An excess of generalisation occurs when you are oriented towards one particular detail which is indeed present in a situation, and you react to its presence, even though the situation is 'totally' or essentially different. You react even though it is not necessary.

Is a toilet not a toilet?

When all details are considered to be equally important, they must not change. For, indeed, when a detail suddenly changes or is no longer present, then the situation itself is no longer the same. Your wearing a blue sweater instead of a green one is for people without autism a mere difference in detail. What is essential – you the person – does not change. You may look a bit different but you are the same. For people that are oriented towards the literal observation of concrete, external details, reality is different.

> Two carpenters are at work in a carpentry shop. One loses his ear in an accident. The other goes searching around and finds the ear. His injured partner says: 'No, that isn't mine. Mine had a pencil stuck to it.'

Individuals with autism fail to grasp the essence of situations. Their understanding is more analytically oriented: every situation is the sum of all details. Like the computer. When I instruct the word processor in my computer to change the abbreviation 'F.A.A.' to 'Flemish Autistic Association', it will not happen where F.A.A. is spelled 'FAA'. The first time this surprised me. Is FAA not the same as F.A.A.? Full stops or no full stops, what's the difference? In terms of meaning there is no difference but my PC doesn't see it that way. It operates literally and analytically, detail by detail. To my PC, dots are as important as letters. To the machine F.A.A. is not the same as FAA because it 'looks' different, and it ignores my instruction. Every detail must be present. FAA is not the same as

F.A.A., 'connection' is not the same as 'connexion', 'organisation' is not the same as 'organization', a 'toilet seat' is not the same as 'lavatory seat'.

> At a camp for children with autism, a boy refused to go to the toilet. Whenever the assistant told him, 'Come on, Mark, go to the toilet,' the boy became scared. He resisted and refused to enter the toilet. All toilets were tried but no result. The boy's parents were consulted. Did Mark do the same at home? Was he sick? Why didn't he want to go to the toilet? The solution was not an easy one. The assistants thought of 'going to the toilet' as a normal, recognisable situation: is not a toilet a toilet? Or maybe not? Yes, it is the same for coherent thinkers but not for someone like Mark who cannot make a distinction between important and non-important details. The assistant went looking for details. Once again, the parents were called. 'What does the toilet at home look like?' 'And the one at school?' After a number of telephone calls, all dealing extensively with every aspect of the toilets, their colours and shapes, the mystery was solved. At home and at school, all the toilets had white seats. The toilet seats at the camp were all black. Mark could not recognise the toilet as a toilet. Something with a black seat is not a toilet! And these assistants are telling him he has to go there to relieve himself!

For us, the colour of the toilet is not important. When you have 'to go', it matters little whether you sit on black or on white. (What counts more for us is that the toilet is kept clean.) But for Mark, the colour was one of the many equally important details.

(You're probably wondering what sort of practical solution we found to this problem? We were in luck: the toilet paper was white, so we wrapped the seat in strips of white paper and that was the end of it.)

The mystery of the toilet paper has a name in literature on autism: resistance to changes.

Ellen is upset when one day dinner is served with blue-handled cutlery. Until then, that cutlery had been used only for meals at the kitchen table. In the dining room, only the silver set was ever used. Ellen replaces the blue cutlery on the table with the silver cutlery.

Max is sent to the kitchen to fetch the mayonnaise. Confused, he keeps standing in front of the open fridge, not being able to find the mayonnaise jar, which is in fact right in front of his eyes. However…this is a different brand to the one the family has always used. Another brand, another label. And thus not recognisable as mayonnaise: because mayonnaise is a jar with a blue-and-yellow label and white letters that spell 'Hellmann's'.

It does often happen that people with autism are capable of something in one situation but incapable in another. This is understandable when you consider that their behaviour is dependent on the presence or the absence of details. At home, Oscar plays very well with his toys but not so well at his grandma's house. Logical, because grandma's home looks totally different to what he is used to: her carpet, on which he makes his toy cars run, is not the same as the one at home.

Since individuals with autism are detail-oriented, they take hold of the details rather than the (invisible) meanings. They recognise situations by the details, which makes the way the world works predictable: a white toilet seat means using the toilet, the silver cutlery means having dinner in the dining room, the blue cutlery means eating in the kitchen.

The world turns into a surreal, absurd and incomprehensible place when in the dining room the kitchen cutlery is placed on the table. When your hold on things has to be derived from details, it is entirely human if a change in the details causes frustration.

A young man is on the verge of marriage and on the eve of the big event enormously nervous and scared. His father tries to put his mind at ease.

'But, son, I too got married and look how happy I am.'

'Yes, yes,' says the boy, 'but you got married to Mother and I am marrying a stranger.'

Imagine a library without a classification system: no thematic listing, no alphabetical arrangement by author's name. Every new book that comes in is placed on the shelves at random. It would be very frustrating to find a book in such a library. You need to memorise the location of a book on the basis of details: this interesting book about gardening can be found in the second row on the fourth shelf to the left, between the book with the yellow cover and the book about model ships. But what if the yellow book changes its location, or is lent out? Or what if all the books on the fourth shelf are placed somewhere else? Imagine the frustration. Every change, however small, changes the whole library and creates a chaotic situation. As a library user you will not be very happy if a book you are seeking has not been put back in its proper place. And just imagine yourself as the librarian of such a library...

The world of people with autism is a bit like this library without a classification system. Since there is too little cohesion and order, details need to remain unchanged.

The orientation towards details does, however, have its advantages: every coin has two sides. External changes to details create new situations for people with autism. This sometimes means that they do not fall back on routines that have grown out of the connection of behaviour to concrete details. This may give rise to a spontaneous behaviour which the person in question had never before used in that particular context. For us, meals are recognisable independent of their details: the colour of cutlery, shape and colour of the table, the type of table settings, the placement...it doesn't make much difference. A meal at a restaurant is a meal like a meal at home. But because a restaurant doesn't look like home, having a meal there is, for certain people with autism, completely different from having one at home. And thus it happens that children at a restaurant suddenly consent to eat their soup, while they have steadfastly refused to do so at home.

Applefries

Another result of hyper-selectivity is over-generalisation. People with autism often connect a certain behaviour to a certain detail. When that detail is observed, they carry out the action that goes with it, regardless of whether this action is called for or not in the context of the situation. When they hear a starter pistol go off, they start running, even though the race hasn't started yet and the starter is only testing out his pistol. Detail thinkers such as people with autism react to external details, not to the meaning or the idea behind the situation. If the detail is identical, even though the situation is different, they react in the accustomed way.

> Daughter: Every time I ask for a new skirt you give me the same answer.

> Mother: Yes, because it is always the same question.

In preparation for a course in social skills I draw up an agenda for the participants. Since people with autism are assisted greatly by concrete and visual communication, I use drawings to support the written language. I store a file with hundreds of drawings in my PC, a handy source of help. As I do not know the name of all of these drawings, I use the search function that is connected to the file. It selects drawings on the basis of key words. I type the word 'locks' in the computer and am presented with the following selections: key locks, building blocks, canal locks, wall clocks… My PC gave me too many drawings: the programme's search function reacts to the literal observation of details, not to the meaning of the key words. The computer gave me all drawings that contain the word 'lock', including building blocks and wall clocks.

> Liz, a girl with autism, had learned at home to peel potatoes and to slice them up. At her school, a birthday party was held for one

of the children. All children would help to bake an apple pie. The teacher knew that Liz could use a knife and gave her the task of peeling and cutting up the apples. Liz peeled her first apple and started to cut it up, just like a potato. The teacher noticed this and showed Liz how to cut apples for an apple pie, in thin slices. Liz did this perfectly and cut up the apple in thin slices. The following day, Liz's mother asked her, as she did frequently, to cut up potatoes for the evening meal. To her amazement, Liz cut up the potatoes in thin slices like apples.

When people with autism are confronted with a new situation, they tend to fall back on familiar routines and already imbedded experiences. Linking behaviour to details is effective in a number of situations, and people with autism can thereby add quite a lot to their existing knowledge. But many situations demand a flexible reaction and flexibility is not generally present in people with autism. Flexibility is generated by the observation of meaning, not of details. Flexibility demands creativity. Learning rules – meaning linking behaviour to details (when you see this…you do that…) – can greatly help individuals with autism but not prevent them from over- and underreacting.

The starting pistol's signal is a part of the race

Focusing on the details does not just influence the reactions of people with autism to situations, it can be used to help them learn about behaviour and conduct. When individuals with autism learn to act in a certain situation, they do not learn this as a cohesive whole made up of separate parts, but rather as a sequence of details that are all equally important. As they do not possess the capacity for overview and classification, as they are incapable of separating the important from the unimportant, quite frequently they are unable to make the distinction between instruction or assistance to an action and the execution of the action itself. For example, when a boy without autism learns to dress himself and his mother assists by telling him what he needs to do and by helping him physically, he understands that this sort of assistance is not part of the act of getting dressed but just a temporary addition to it. He is capable of putting his world in the right order and thus draws a clear distinction between 'the act of dressing' and the 'assistance in the act of dressing'.

- Mummy helps me in putting my feet through my trouser legs (assistance).
- Mummy says: 'Now pull up your trousers' (instruction).
- I pull up my trousers (this is part of the act of getting dressed).

People with autism cannot always make this distinction. The result is that both the instructions and the various steps in the activity are all regarded as equally important parts of the action. To get dressed thus consists of:

- Mummy pulls my feet through the trouser legs.
- Mummy says: 'Now pull up your trousers'.
- I pull up my trousers.
- Mummy says: 'Very well done.'

If you happen to remove one of these details, the whole is no longer the action of 'dressing oneself'. That is the way it works with individuals with autism. If Mummy stops giving instruction after she has helped pull his feet through the trouser legs, the boy doesn't know what to do any more. The sequence of details has been ruptured. It is no longer 'getting dressed' because Mummy has to say: 'Now pull up your trousers'.

Just as computers are dependent on individual instructions for the processing of detailed instructions, so people with autism become readily dependent on commands and instructions.

The boy waits to pull up his trousers until his mother gives the order. The sentence 'Now pull up your trousers' has become an essential part of the act of getting dressed. Individuals with autism often get going only after the starting pistol has been fired. The pistol shot belongs to the race.

There is a difficult term to explain this phenomenon. It is said that individuals with autism are 'person dependent' (when they have need of spoken instructions) or 'structure dependent' (when they need photos, pictures, material that is prepared and similar things). In fact, it is treating the same thing twice. Both are forms of 'instruction-dependency'.[2] Just as with computers, it often happens that people with autism fail to execute tasks when hints are absent, when the right key is not pushed, when they are not given a push in the right direction.

> A boy with autism was taught how to brush his teeth. His mother had shown him with pictures the various stages he had to pass through. It went OK, only the spitting out didn't work so well. To help him, Tom's mother gave him a light tap on the head and said 'spit it out, Tom'. Tom reacted immediately. This went on for some time. Tom just didn't manage to go through the whole process of brushing his teeth on his own. He kept getting stuck with the water for rinsing in his mouth. He was waiting for the knock on his head. This had become for him part of the process. He needed it as part of brushing his teeth.

Brushing teeth represented for Tom:

- …

- I put down my toothbrush
- I take my glass of water
- I take a gulp of water
- I receive a knock on my head
- I spit out the water

- …

Tom literally needed that knock on the head before he could get into action. As long as the command did not come, he didn't react

– just like another boy who kept running around with chewing gum in his mouth and really wanted to get rid of it, but he had only been told 'not to swallow it'.

People with autism deal with reality very literally and very rigidly. Whether it pertains to social situations, communications or everyday activities – such as brushing their teeth, getting dressed, or going to the toilet – they are more or less blind to the spirit or essence of what is happening. And because of it, they react strangely, comically and non-flexibly. Their behaviour can in fact resemble the behaviour of an automaton.

Even in ordinary situations those with autism are confronted with problems. Like other people they try to solve these problems but because they approach things from a literal point of view, they come up with different solutions.

Notes

1.   Momma (1996, p.101).

2.   Person dependency is frequently manifested in more intelligent people with autism
      or people with more subtle expressions of autism. Because of their greater orienta-
      tion towards others, they turn to people when they are at a loss as to what to do.
      They hold fast to others when the environment has become too vague and implicit.
      Less intelligent people with autism or people with more severe, classic forms of au-
      tism tend to be more dependent on certain objects than certain persons, although
      they can be person dependent too. The form differs but, in essence, all people with
      autism are very dependent on instruction and clarification. See Vermeulen (1999).

CHAPTER 7

Making Coffee is Not a 2 + 2 Problem

About problems and problem solving

There is a big difference between the theoretical knowledge of facts and 'common sense'. In the case of the knowledge of facts, cohesive thinking is barely required. A good memory will get you a long way. But cohesive thinking is especially useful in solving everyday problems. Memorising the whole train schedule doesn't mean you will be able to catch the train on your own. Knowing the names of objects won't make it easier for you to use them. People with autism may have a very extensive theoretical knowledge of things. However, their common sense is often not developed enough to allow them to tackle simple domestic problems for which we, without much thought, find fast and simple solutions.

Since the external world does not always make a lot of sense to them, people with autism have recourse to concrete instructions and rules. Recognising the rational or the irrational in certain activities or in the solution of a problem is what common sense is for. And it requires a feel for context, which is not measurable. Sense and nonsense have nothing to do with details, rules or logic. But what is true or false, correct or incorrect, is tied to the rules of logic. People with autism can often distinguish between the correct and the incorrect, the true and the false, and they see truth and correctness as very important factors in their lives. But to know whether something makes sense or not, that is much more of a problem. Sense and nonsense flow out of the coherence of things and events. Coherence results from discovering meaning. And this cohesion cannot be grasped by the rules of logic.

Autism is thus not just a problem of assigning meaning; it is a problem of assigning sense. People with autism experience problems in making sense out of things because they have insufficient understanding of the coherence and meaning of things that make sense.[1] For that reason, individuals with autism have difficulties in solving problems efficiently and effectively; they miss the main point.

Effectiveness and efficiency

Being effective means attempting a task with a well thought-out purpose in mind. But how can you work effectively if you neither grasp the purpose of an activity nor understand it fully? People with autism are much less purposeful in their actions.

People who work efficiently don't simply proceed helter-skelter: they need to be selective in what they do in order to reach their goals. But how can you be efficient if you cannot judge an action in terms of its cohesion with the objective you want to achieve? People with autism are much less goal-oriented. They have difficulties in solving problems, even simple ones, because they are less purposeful and less goal-oriented.

But there is more. If you want to be effective and efficient, you must be able to look beyond the details. You need to take an overview of the whole and be flexible enough to assign details their place in the whole picture, which is forever changing.

If you want to get to Bristol, it won't help you to sing folk songs from Bristol. That is not being effective. You have to get into your car and drive to Bristol. That is effective. But it is not, in itself, efficient. You can get to Bristol in different ways. If you leave from London and you proceed via Gloucester, it might be effective (you can get to Bristol via Gloucester) but it is hardly efficient since you are making quite a detour. The road via Reading is shorter and thus more efficient. But not always. If you want to get to Bristol from Birmingham, then Gloucester is the most efficient route and Reading is the detour. Sometimes, driving via Gloucester can be more efficient than via Reading, even from London – if, say, the M4 was closed to traffic for one reason or another.

Efficiency and effectiveness have to do with flexibility: you don't always act in a pre-set and rigid manner but remain open to adaptation depending on changing circumstances, as the context demands. You don't always take the rules literally but you adapt them in the way that makes the best sense – unlike Sally, who heard at school that one should brush one's teeth three times a day. Next day she brushed her teeth three times – right after dinner, three times in a row.

People with autism are less flexible. Once they have mastered an activity, they will perform it literally and identically, all steps and details neatly in the order they have been taught. As long as the situation does not change, it remains effective. Alas, situations do change (sometimes there is a traffic jam on the M4) and at such times you have to be able to adapt what you have learned. If you cannot master this, some strange things may occur.

> One morning, a woman standing on her balcony notices the arrival of two men from the Municipal Parks Department. One begins to dig a hole by the road while the other watches. When the first one has finished, the other begins to fill the hole. When the hole is filled in, he neatly levels the soil. This continues all morning: one digs holes, the other fills them and levels the soil. The woman is fascinated by what is happening and decides to ask the men what they are doing. One tells her: 'Well, the problem lies with Tony. He's sick and he's the one who has to plant the trees.'

> A young man with autism[2] had been taught at the institution where he lived how to do the laundry: first put everything in the

washing machine, then in the dryer. He did this every week, before going home for the weekend. One weekend he came home with a suitcase full of wet clothes. He had followed the laundry routine all right: first put the clothes into the washing machine, push the button, when the machine stops, take out the clothes and put them in the dryer, push the button, wait for the signal that indicates the end of the drying cycle, take out the clothes, fold the clothes and put them in the suitcase. Alas, that week there was a problem with the dryer: the machine didn't work even though it still gave the signal. The young man had learned all the steps but he had failed to grasp the real meaning of the activity (drying the clothes).

The doctor writes out a prescription and hands it to the patient: 'Rub your chest with this three times a day.'

After a week the patient is back.

The doctor asks, 'And did it help?'

The patient replies, 'Yes, thank you, Doctor, but can you give me another piece of paper? Maybe a bit bigger because the one you gave me became shredded after just two days of rubbing.'

People with autism get hung up on certain activities, even after these have become useless or superfluous because the context and thus the meaning has changed. In other words, after they have lost their effectiveness.

Detail thinkers like people with autism cannot adapt their behaviour properly to the changing contexts. They go through activities and routines as though they are events that exist on their own, isolated from any meaning and without connection to the context.

The Albanian President was visiting Belgium. On the way from the airport to his hotel he noticed that lines had been painted in the middle of the road. He asked the Belgian Prime Minister about the purpose of the lines. The Prime Minister explained that they served to keep traffic in the correct lanes, something which the Albanian President thought was a splendid idea. Finally he had found a solution to the traffic chaos in his country.

Back in Albania he called the Minister of Transport and Highways and told him to put his best workman on the job. The road from the presidential residence to the airport would be the first to get the treatment. Paint and paint brushes were ready.

The following day, the workman started his paint job. In the evening, the President went to take a look. Two kilometres of road had been painted. Satisfied, the President went home. The next day, only an additional 1 kilometre had been painted, and the day after, only 500 metres more. When the President asked the reason for this, the workman answered: 'But Mr President, it's a long way back and forth to the paint can.'

Thomas, a young man with autism, has to make his bed. He is not yet able to do this and I give him a hand. I show Thomas how to put down the bottom sheet. Together with me, he tucks in the four sides of the bottom sheet under the mattress so that it looks taut and smooth all around. Then I leave the room, giving Thomas the instruction to finish making the bed. After a while I return. Thomas has made the bed perfectly. The only thing is, the upper sheet and the blanket too have been tucked in along all four sides.

Thomas does not see the total picture of 'making the bed' and gets hung up on the activity he has been taught. He does not comprehend that later on he will also have to climb 'into' the bed, between the sheets, even though that is what beds are for. He reacts surprised when I ask him: 'How are you going to get into bed?' Only then does Thomas see that he has made a mistake, observing: 'Wow, you're a smart guy. Went to university?'

More like bureaucrats than strategists: Rituals

Like the lack of flexibility in solving daily problems – indeed, a product of it – ritualistic behaviour is not uncommon in people with autism. What originally was a functional and efficient solution assumes a life of its own. The activity is performed even though it doesn't make sense (any longer).

> 'Tell me, boss, these files are cluttering up the place; can we burn them?'
>
> 'Yes, I suppose so. But just in case, make a photocopy of them beforehand.'

> Ben has learned to put his slippers on when he enters the bathroom. One day, the family goes swimming. Ben notices he has left his hairbrush behind. While the whole family waits in the car, Ben runs upstairs. He removes his shoes and puts on his slippers. Then he goes inside the bathroom to fetch his hairbrush. Then he takes his slippers off and puts his shoes back on. In total, fetching his hairbrush takes some five minutes, and in the meantime the family sits waiting in the car.

People with autism cling to ritualistic or automatic behaviour (this is called stereotyping), because it offers them security and is comfortable. It is unchanging; everything else changes and is thus unpredictable.

Coherent thinkers consider ritual activity 'pointless', because of its absence of relationship with the ultimate goal. To us, rituals are sources of frustration. Parents and counsellors often need 'to wait' for an individual with autism because he or she is 'going through' a ritual that for cohesive thinkers is just superfluous and a waste of time. Why does he have to blow his nose once more, when we are in such a hurry? He just did it a second ago…

However, people with autism do not consider these rituals or stereotypes as being senseless – they offer security. Furthermore, the activities of people with autism are rather like a fixed sequence of actions, a series of separate steps that need to be taken one by one, an absolute procedure. 'This is the way it happens to be. This is the way it must be.'

> Anne is very precise and orderly. Whenever she takes something from her toiletry bag, she closes it immediately afterwards. Brushing her teeth and washing her hands thus involves: opening the bag, taking out the toothbrush and the toothpaste, closing the bag, putting toothpaste on the toothbrush, opening the bag, putting the toothpaste inside, closing the bag, and so on.

For the person who looks at the whole picture, this ritual of opening and closing the toiletry bag is pointless. But this is not the way Anne looks at it. She does not see the whole picture. Every step she takes (taking out the toothbrush and the paste, squeezing the paste onto the brush, brushing her teeth) is a separate activity. And after every activity, you close the bag.

Because they do not see the whole picture, people with autism abhor interruptions in procedure. People without autism see the guiding thread through all the various steps that make up an activity. After an interruption, they just pick up the thread where they left off. Not so people with autism: because they do not see the whole, they lose the thread whenever an interruption happens. Thus, they have to start again from the beginning. In the words of a man with autism: 'It is important that, when the chain of decisions has been interrupted by an external cause, a new start be made from the very beginning. Because of the process of over-selectivity, everything literally has changed.'[3]

> Simon, a young man with autism, once couldn't get out of bed, he felt so tired and stiff. He was told it would help if he stretched his muscles before getting up. This he did and it had the desired effect. Simon likes physical exercise and wants to be handsome and strong. Now it takes him over two hours to get out of bed. He doesn't get up until all his muscles have been stretched. This

has to happen every morning, even when he doesn't feel tired.
He does not want to miss even one of his exercises and when he is
interrupted he simply starts from the beginning.

Detail thinkers solve problems in (from our viewpoint) absurd and
senseless ways because they do not fully grasp cohesion and fail to
see the whole picture. Activities are isolated instances. Anne,
Simon and Ben have difficulties integrating activities into a
coherent whole because they are deficient in grasping the meaning
of situations and miss the context in which activities are combined
and grouped together. And when activities cannot be incorporated
in a sensible (purposeful) context, they become isolated routines or
rituals, free-standing as it were.

Individuals with autism display little strategy in their actions.[4]
We call somebody strategically oriented when she can adjust
herself readily to changing problematic situations and can think of
'made-to-measure' solutions that are adapted to the meaning or
the sense of the situation. Procedures, on the contrary, refer to
fixed rules. They are 'laid down' and offer a foothold. They are
there to be executed.

The routines followed by Anne, Simon and Ben call to mind the
stereotype of the public bureaucrat. He too follows procedures,
isolated from all context and to the great annoyance of the person
on the other end of the telephone. ('It cannot be done without
Form B20,' he says, even though it's just a question of asking the
boss to move his car.) People with autism resemble bureaucrats
more than strategists.

'And just repeat the same thing'

When we, coherent thinkers, find ourselves confronted with a
problem, we do not always find the solution on our own. Even the
best strategists need to go and seek some help. Often we consult
others who have already found a solution and then imitate them:
we have recourse to copy-catting. But even in copy-catting you

have to be sensitive to meanings and look at the whole context.[5] What needs to be imitated is, intuitively, taken from the context. People who lack that intuition either cannot imitate or do so incorrectly.

An older couple intend to travel by train for the first time.

'How do I get a ticket?' the man asks.

'Go and stand in the queue, listen to the person in front and do the same,' his wife replies.

He waits in the queue until he is almost at the ticket office. The traveller in front says: 'One return ticket for Peterlee.'

Then it is the old man's turn: 'One return ticket for Joseph Miller,' he says.

Steven is going to play bingo, but he doesn't quite understand what to do. He stacks his cards. The assistant shows Steven how to place the cards on the main board and urges him to imitate her. After a few tries he gets the idea. He places the cards on the board. However, because he hasn't entirely grasped that the cards need to be placed on the identical pictures on the main board, the assistant helps him with this. She taps the spot where the card has to be put down. And Steven does the same…he too taps the spot on the board.

We find simple imitation exercises easy to do, because we pick up from the context what needs to be imitated and filter out what doesn't. But somebody who lacks this intuitive feeling has more difficulty with this.

What, in fact, do you do in the following situation?

'Do this!'

Figure 7.1

What do you need to do? It seems simple but there are a couple of possibilities...

Figure 7.2

If you don't know what is 'meant' by 'this', chances are that you will imitate what is not demanded. Failure to understand meanings can have far-reaching consequences and may lead to strange behaviour in problem-solving activities, even when the solution may seem obvious to others.

A man comes home from the tailor's wearing his new suit.

His wife: And did you do what I told you? Did you order two pairs of trousers?

He: Yes, but to be honest, it feels a bit warm on my legs.

During a lesson about multiplication with 2 (doubling), the teacher explained some points on the blackboard. She wrote a number on the left side, and to the right of it the double of that number. Next she drew an arrow from the one number to the other and wrote along it: 'x 2'. She then gave this step a name, calling it 'doubling'. After she had done this a few times, she wrote the numbers 4 and 8 on the blackboard. She asked Jessy, a girl with autism: 'Jessy, what do you have to do to go from 4 to 8?' Jessy answered: 'Draw an arrow.'

It is common for people with autism to carry out activities or instructions without knowing the purpose, the meaning, of the action.

This is also the case with computers. As commanded by the operator, they execute calculations but do not know the purpose of these 'calculations'. Computers don't ask questions about the 'why' of their actions. And they lack the ability to look back on their own actions and to search for their meaning. A number of very 'smart' computers exist that can tell you why they are carrying out certain calculations or actions but if you keep on probing more deeply after the 'why' you will ultimately receive an answer something like 'because you told me to do it', or, 'because my program is written that way'. Or, as in the conversation between a girl and a computer in the bestseller *Sophie's World*:[6]

Sophie keys in: 'Who is Hilde Moller Knag?'

'Hilde Moller Knag lives in Lillesand and is the same age as Sophie Amundsen.'

'How do you know that?'

'I don't know how I know that. It's on my hard disk.'

Like computers, individuals with autism, given clear instructions, will carry them out to the letter but often without knowing their significance or purpose. They carry out functions without understanding what it is they are doing. Individuals with autism are a bit like the first monks who were copying texts. They were first-class calligraphers – copying perfect letters and drawing decorative illustrations – but they were totally ignorant of the meaning of what they were copying…they were illiterate.

> Mary, a girl with autism, is making a mess of her dinner. Her whole person, her chair, the table, everything is covered in chocolate milk. Her father finally runs out of patience and says: 'Enough, go and eat your sandwich in the hall.' When her mother comes home a little later and hears the whole story, she asks Mary: 'And why were you in the hall?'
>
> Mary answers: 'To eat my sandwich.'
>
> 'And why did you have to eat your sandwich in the hall?'
>
> 'Because Daddy told me to.'

Without elaborating further, this anecdote makes it clear how difficult it is for persons with autism to 'learn' from their experiences and of how little effect punishment is on detail thinkers. This is because they do not really understand the coherence in and the consequences of their actions. Children with autism generally experience difficulties accepting criticism because of that very problem. Criticism is like a thunderclap out of a clear sky. And when they understand the 'why' of the punishment, they remain almost always blind to its purpose. For that reason, punishment very seldom results in behavioural changes in individuals with autism.

To make coffee is not 2 + 2. Decision making is more than calculating

Individuals with autism are very good at doing as they are asked, but they do so 'robotically' (a bit like computers), rigidly and by the book (a bit like officious bureaucrats) – without much flexibility.

Being flexible in solving problems presupposes making decisions, something which is not so easy for persons with autism. How do you proceed, cutting or slicing? Will you be given potatoes or apples? And if it is potatoes, do they need to be cut in chunks? (Coherent thinkers have already made the decision on the basis of the context. They have seen the frying pan and know that the potatoes need to be cut in strips and not in chunks. The exact instruction need not be given to them.) How thick should the potato strips be?

We don't think twice about the many decisions that need to be made in the performance of our daily tasks. Coherent thinkers make many decisions intuitively, since it is obvious from the associations between things what needs to be done and what can happen. As it were, we 'feel' all of that.

In the following instruction, most people spontaneously know what sort of glass they need to find and empty: 'find a glass of water that is fuller than the one you are holding and drink it until it is empty'.

People with autism have difficulties making decisions. Some people with autism, who have normal or high intelligence, try to *calculate* solutions to their problems, like a computer. But they are immediately confronted with the fact that many of our human problems cannot be approached from a mathematical base: aesthetics, religion, emotional conflicts – these cannot be treated by mere calculations.

A computer can provide you unfailingly with data about all works of art in the world, where they are found, when they were made, by whom, what their sizes are, and so on. It can store all these facts inside its memory and apply calculations and processes to them. If you want to know the exact location of all the Gaudí buildings in Barcelona, or you want to find which Flemish primitives are hanging in the Louvre, a computer will give you the answers within seconds.

But if you want to take a stroll around the museums in Paris and you ask the computer to give you an idea of what works of art are 'splendid', you can't really expect an answer. At best, you may receive a list of all art that somehow features the word 'splendid' in its description or in its title, such as: 'most tourists agree that this is indeed a splendid work of art'.

But even where it concerns everyday ordinary things, calculating and reasoning it out may not help much. 'Deductive reasoning is not suitable for most "real-life" situations. There are too many things to take into account simultaneously to be able to rely solely on reasoning.'[7]

To tackle trivial domestic problems demands another kind of intelligence to that needed for solving mathematical puzzles. Making coffee is not the same as adding 2 + 2, nor is how you react to a red traffic light. They are not problems thet can be solved by a multiplication table or by taking square roots.

To solve mathematical problems all you need to know are the mathematical rules and procedures. Once you have mastered these, 2 + 2 always make 4. Wherever you may be (in class, at home, in a café), in whatever form the assignment is given ('two plus two' or '2 + 2'), whoever is giving the assignment (the teacher, aunt Irma, or the neighbour's daughter), all you need to do is apply the formula and the problem is solved. These formulae are called algorithms, and the mathematical problems they address are uniform and unambiguous. If you do this, then do that, then do this and then do such-and-such you'll get there. No doubt.

Making coffee, however, is a different proposition. To make coffee, as for other everyday activities, there are no algorithms to fall back on. There are, however, a number of rules to apply. You know you have to put a filter paper in the filter before adding the ground coffee, and that the machine should really be plugged in if you want it to work. But for other parts of the coffee-making process there are no clear rules. It makes little difference if you fill the water receptacle before you pour the ground coffee into the filter or vice versa (but this does not mean putting the ground coffee into the water receptacle and water into the filter!). In addition, the quantity of ground coffee you use can depend on the preference of the person who is going to drink it (this person likes strong coffee, the other not). It will also differ according to the kind of coffee pot you use (pots with an anti-drip system require the lid on top, others do not).

Furthermore, and this is the greatest difference with mathematical problems, these everyday human problems may demand that you take into account the cohesion that exists between things, external influences such as, for instance, toddlers, wine decanters, glass fragments and vacuum cleaners. These are the factors you cannot calculate. They are 'incalculable', meaning unpredictable.

Now imagine this situation. While you are preparing the coffee, you notice that the pot is empty. In order to get to the coffee jar, you need to put aside a glass decanter. It drops from your grasp and shatters in a thousand pieces on the floor. This presents a danger for the toddler in the house, which forces you to pick up the fragments. The largest pieces you can gather by hand. But for the tiny almost invisible slivers you need a vacuum cleaner.

People with autism can solve daily problems quite well, as long as there exist clear rules and procedures, and on the condition that they have learned such rules and routines. Making coffee generally does not present a problem, until that day when the coffee pot is empty and the glass decanter slips from their grasp and drops to the floor.

People with autism can often describe the rules very well. It is not at all uncommon for children with autism to find the perfect solution to a test problem. And if you ask them to describe the procedure for making coffee, they will go through all the steps in detailed order. But…in real life it is not that easy. It is not because you have learned to draw the map of a town that you know it.

This is very confusing for the parents. But it does become somewhat more understandable when you know that in a test situation there need be no consideration for incalculable factors such as toddlers, glass fragments and vacuum cleaners.

Much more than for people without autism, those with autism rely on clear rules in order to find solutions to problems. Depending on the degree of their intelligence, they can learn a large number of rules, master them or even calculate them. Normal situations therefore do not present major difficulties. It is when things cannot be calculated that they run up against a brick wall. To react flexibly in the face of these incalculable elements is problematic for individuals with autism.

> Betty, a young lady with autism who helps clean company premises, is told one day to clean the stairs. As a result she goes into a monologue, talking aloud to herself. She can't decide whether to start at the top of the stairs or at the bottom. She musters all sorts of arguments for and against but finds no ideal starting point for this job of cleaning the stairs. This cannot be calculated. So much depends on so many incalculable factors. Ultimately, somebody else will have to tell her how to proceed.

Real problem solving has to do more with guesswork and intuition than with calculations, and guesswork and intuitive reacting are not easy for people with autism. They want clear rules, unambiguous procedures. They want clear, external, logical criteria rather than vague, internal and intuitive ones.

> Kevin, a young man with autism, works in a company as an office boy. He assists with the mail, does photocopying, occasionally enters data into the computer. But even a simple copying job requires a number of difficult decisions:
>
> - How many copies are needed of the original?
> - Do the copies need to be collated?
> - Does he need to copy one side or both sides?
> - What colour ink is required? (Black, blue? The copier can also make colour copies.)

- Does he need to attach the copied pages to each other? With a stapler or only with a paper clip? Where should he attach the staple? At the top right or the left? What sort of staples should he use? (Copper ones or the ordinary kind?)

- Where do the copies go? (In the mail slots? Back to the office that ordered them? In an envelope?)

These are not complex questions and answering them is simple for those without autism. When the assignment is clear enough, Kevin will succeed. The copying will be carried out as requested if clear instructions on how to proceed are given to Kevin in advance: 'Kevin, I need five copies of this document in black ink, both sides, collated and stapled with an ordinary staple top left. Return the original and the copies to me.'

> But then there are still more decisions. How clear do the copies need to be? If something shows up a bit grey, is that OK? If the page is incomplete, where do you put the original: at the top of the glass plate? At the bottom? Or do you centre it? If there are five pages in total to be copied as a double-sided document, which page will have only the front side? The first? The last? Or another? And what if the original sheet shifts a bit and the copy is a little askew? Is it necessary to make another copy? Do the copies have to be faultless copies? How faultless is faultless?

> Sometimes, Kevin is in grave doubt in front of his photocopier. Sometimes he takes 20 sample copies to find the right position of the text on the page (clear, measurable, external criterion), while the main factor for the employees is not the external appearance but the content of the document (the internal aspect rather than the form).

Embarrassment of riches[8]

If he needs to take a decision about copying a document, Kevin has a great deal of difficulty in making a pre-selection amongst possible alternatives. It thus takes him a while to reach a conclusion. All the possible arguments pass through his mind and he experiences difficulties in putting them in a certain order. He considers the ecological argument (too much sampling wastes too much paper and is thus harmful to the environment), the aesthetic one (if it is not properly centred it doesn't look nice), the practical one (if it isn't black enough then the text will not be very legible), and…and…

People with autism labour mightily with the process of decision making, much more than other people do. They therefore require much more time. Making decisions is being selective, choosing what is important, sensible or useful and what is not. Making choices is often a horrendous task for persons with autism. As they lack feeling for the cohesion of things, no pre-selecting of alternatives takes place: this means that when they are required to make choices, they see themselves confronted with a host of possible alternatives, as well as with those alternatives that coherent thinkers have eliminated beforehand because they do not fit into the context of the whole.

It is bitterly cold outside and snowing. You are standing before your wardrobe trying to decide what to wear. Given the context, you can immediately eliminate a large number of possibilities: your shorts, cotton shirts, light socks, summer sandals, summer jacket – there is no debate about these. The alternatives for your choice are warm winter clothes.

A person with autism sees it differently. If you were to ask him: 'what are you going to wear today?' he pictures to himself the whole wardrobe. And while he may realise that on a cold winter's day you don't go out in shorts and summer sandals, for every piece of garment the decision needs to be taken anew – and this includes the summer clothes. Even something as pedestrian as selecting what to wear is a slow and tedious process for someone with autism. And being slow does not mean being lazy either.

Not being able to carry out pre-selections leads in addition to ravioli-responses and washbasin reasoning. People without autism follow instructions from the standpoint of context (the subject concerns a doll's bed) and for that reason begin by excluding quite a number of answer-categories: foodstuffs (such as ravioli) don't belong here, nor are office items (such as stamps) appropriate; we must search in the category of bed-articles. Without this pre-selection, a much larger number of categories has to be considered and it is therefore quite logical that the first similar item that pops up will lead to an answer – even though the answer may originate in a wrong category.

People without autism insist on choosing and making their own decisions; it is their right, the cornerstone of their freedom. For people with autism, making choices and decisions is like an imposition with which they are confronted. Freedom of choice is experienced by them less commonly as a right than as a difficult, sometimes all too heavy, burden. Life for them is much easier when there are clear rules and when others carry out the pre-selections, so that making decisions may turn into a feasible proposition for them.

Notes

1.   The word 'sense' signifies different things, primarily 'meaning', such as in: 'What is the meaning of this pronouncement?' But it also means 'purpose': 'What purpose is there in going fishing in your leisure time?' Autism is a problem of 'sense' in both these meanings. People with autism have difficulty in assigning meaning to things, but they have even more difficulty in understanding the purpose behind things and happenings.

2.   The example is taken from Hart (1989).

3.   Van Dalen (1995a, p.14).

4.   The problems that people with autism experience in acting strategically (planning, inspecting and evaluating actions) have led to a cognitive theory in the explanation of autism whereby it is held that autism is the result of a deficit in the 'executive function'. To find out more about this concept, please refer to, amongst others, Hughes, Russell and Robbins (1994) and Ozonoff (1995).

5.   Studies have shown that the development of copy-catting in ordinary children is linked to their understanding of 'purpose' (Hay *et al.* 1991).

6.   Jostein Gaarder (1994, p.265).

7.   Hofstadter (1979). The quote is taken from the Dutch translation, 1985, p.649. Deductive reasoning extracts, via logical reasoning, more specific rules from general ones. The opposite of this is 'inductive reasoning'. In inductive reasoning, one arrives at a more general rule on the basis of some similar situations. People with autism are probably better in deductive reasoning, but more studies are needed to confirm this.

8.   This expression refers to having too many choices.

CHAPTER 8

Between the Lines
About autistic intelligence (2)

Intelligence: To have or to have not

> 'Every happening appears in some inevitable way to impose itself upon them: people with autism are not good at concentrating their attention and they "lose their way" inside the host of stimuli.'[1]

People with autism seem to be the playthings of events, of a series of unstoppable isolated happenings, a bombardment of details. Their world is a fragmented world, a 'multiversum' from which cohesion and order is absent. In the word of a person with autism: 'I compare autistic sight with the faceted vision of an insect: a host of different subtle details but all of it non-integrated.'[2]

Central coherence, the ability to establish cohesion, is not something you are either born with or not. It is an ability that is developed, something people can acquire to a greater or lesser degree. It is wrong to think that people with autism entirely lack central coherence. It's just that with them the ability is weakly developed: to further complicate things the degree of weakness of central coherence is not identical in all individuals with autism.

Very young children, autistic or not, detect little cohesion in their environment. They are not yet able to make the required distinction between themselves and the outside world. Their experiences are not yet their own. Like people with autism, they do not interpret things as 'happening to themselves'. There is still too little 'I', too little personality and self-consciousness. They differ very little from people with autism.

But the difference does come in time. Non-autistic children are born with the ability to gradually come to experience coherence. Their brains command a central control unit where the transformation into personality is being formed. Gradually, they change into individuals. The word 'individual' is derived from the Latin and signifies 'indivisible'. Taking the place of many loose experiences is one single whole unit, a coherent entity: a person who can integrate many experiences in his life into a rational and indivisible whole – 'I'![3]

In individuals with autism, central coherence is insufficiently developed. Like computers, they process all information that enters their brain as 'absolute' not as relative data. Input is made up of too many loose details (the word 'absolute' is also derived from the Latin and means 'loose standing'). Information is processed with too little relation made to other information within the context. When you key the word 'hotel' into a computer, the machine processes the word as a combination of the separate letters H-O-T-E-L. The computer does not understand that this unique combination refers to a building where people come to sleep overnight: the computer has absolutely no idea what a hotel is.

Do we thus call people with autism 'dense' or 'dumb' in the way computers are dumb? Is it because of their 'dumbness' that we find them funny? Jokes are often about the 'denseness' of people.

Many people say 'no' to this, for some people with autism have a tremendous gift for figures, for art. They give evidence of a fabulous memory. They manage to cope in a world that makes no sense to them. People with that sort of ability can hardly be labelled 'dumb'.

For a long time – all too long – it was accepted that people with autism were intelligent beings caught in their autistic prison. It was accepted that children with autism, due to a lack of love, were isolating themselves from the normal outside world. Because of the wall they erected around themselves, they became unapproachable and chose barely to react to outside challenges. They appeared dumb, but that was just for show. For, indeed, one was a wizard with figures, another could replay any piece of music after just one hearing. If only we could break through this autistic shell, we would unearth a talented child, a child with all the gifts to blossom forth in marvellous ways.

In the course of time, we have come to know better.[4] Many professionals and parents have come to a complete halt before the very wall they tried to demolish. Trying to cure autism is like fighting windmills. And even where autism does seem to tail off, the expected level of intelligence is not what we thought it would be.

Autism manifests itself on all levels of intelligence. Most people with autism also have a learning disability and are thus doubly disabled. They interpret the world differently because of their autism and understand less of it, because of their low intelligence. Their world is even more limited than that of people with autism who do not possess an intellectual disability. As well as this large group of less gifted people with autism, we find normally endowed people with autism as well as very gifted individuals.

But even these highly gifted individuals with autism miss the boat in some situations. Some of them do not have the social intelligence of a toddler. They may be able to programme a computer but they haven't got a clue about how to fit into a conversation.

The misunderstanding about the talent of people with autism is the result of a mistaken understanding of intelligence. Intelligence is often interpreted wrongly as a kind of 'monolithic block', something that consists of one single block. Intelligence is what you possess in greater or lesser degree: either you are smart or you are dumb. This is really a 'dumb' interpretation since, on the basis of it, people could only be classified in two groups: intelligent or not. And if someone (with autism) is able to do spectacular calculations, she has to be ranked with the intelligent group, in spite of all her shortcomings. This limited interpretation of intelligence gives rise to pointless discussions about 'to have it or not to have it', meaning being intelligent or not being intelligent…

Analysing (the trees) or integrating (the woods)

There is no such thing as *the* intelligence. 'Intelligence' in and of itself is meaningless.[5]

You may have a gift for languages but be a dolt in mathematics. Some people are very good in orienting themselves in a city or a building but lose their way in trying to follow instructions on how to use a video camera. Clearly, there are different kinds of intelligence. Once you see intelligence from this point of view, the question of whether people with autism are intelligent or not intelligent is found to be at fault. The right question is: in what way is the structure of their intelligence different from that of people without autism?[6]

The integrating form of intelligence in particular is less developed in people with autism. This does not mean that people with autism are totally incapable of gathering details into a coherent whole. Sometimes they do succeed in integrating the separate aspects of their observation. But if they do succeed in doing that, they proceed in an entirely different way from people without autism. In this way too, their methods of processing information resemble those of the computer.

Computers process information step by step: serially.[7] All bits of input are processed in a series, one by one and one after the other. Computers cannot process two things simultaneously, unlike the human brain, which processes information in a parallel way.

Like computers, people with autism process information serially. J.G.T. Van Dalen, a man with autism, describes this admirably:[8] when he sees a hammer he needs to process every bit of this information separately and line it up. He does not instantly become aware that this is a hammer. He first sees a piece of metal, then –

attached to it – a piece of wood that looks like a handle. Then he notices that the two pieces are connected and finally he reaches the conclusion that this is a hammer. Step by step he processes the originally unrelated impressions of the parts until they form a whole unit.

People with autism have difficulty dealing with various things at the same time. Information is processed 'piece by piece'; their intelligence is characterised by 'piecemeal processing'. In this, they need time to gain an understanding. We often experience that people with autism have a delayed reaction time. The autistic penny drops more slowly.

The main problem for people with autism lies in their lack of quick, parallel and integrated processing of information. In other areas they may well be more intelligent than people without autism. Just like computers: machines must concede the primacy of people in many fields; however, they can execute most calculations much faster than the human brain.

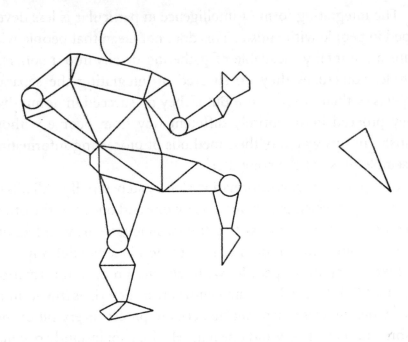

Figure 8.1

In tasks where noticing details is more important than noticing the whole, people with autism perform better than ordinary people. This was demonstrated by the experiments of Beate Hermelin and Neil O'Connor, pioneers in the research of autistic thinking. They showed pictures such as the one above to children with autism and children without autism.[9]

The purpose of this sort of exercise is seeing that the triangle to the right is found in the drawing to the left. Children with autism scored better in this than the other children. Persons without autism need more time to find the triangle in the left drawing because they are concentrating on the whole picture: they see a person. In order to score well on this sort of test, you have to be able to disregard the whole and only look at the details. You need to divorce yourself from the person and look at the drawing as a random collection of lines and shapes.

> A young man with autism, who had helped me for some time with little administrative tasks, effortlessly managed to isolate all the typing mistakes in my texts. I myself was so occupied with content, the meaning of my writings, the whole picture, that I simply read across the typing mistakes. They were just external details. He picked them out in the twinkling of an eye.

Another young man astounded us during a TV quiz evening by identifying tunes after hearing only a couple of notes. In recognising tunes we hear the large picture, the refrain, the melody. For him, a music composition is rather a series of 'notes', a pattern of details. When you have stored a whole series of these patterns in your mind, you can easily identify one of these patterns after just a couple of notes and thus recognise the tune. People with autism make good analysts. Their analytic intelligence is far better developed than their integrating intelligence.

> Judge: Can you give us a detailed description of the attacker?
>
> Witness: He stank of beer.

> Judge: That is not enough. You must give us some more details, please.
>
> Witness: I think it was Guinness.

> Bob, a young man who often participated in our training sessions in social skills, could not only list the exact dates of all courses in the past eight years but also give the names of all the participants. Where a participant had not shown up for a while and then suddenly was present again, Bob could say: 'The last time you were present was during the weekend of 7–9 December, 1992. That was in Antwerp.' Some of our participants can give perfect descriptions of my behaviour during previous activities: 'You did this and you said that…', but found it much less easy to render the *feel* or the atmosphere of a previous activity.

People with autism can be good behaviourists. They can perfectly describe and remember someone's conduct for a long time. People without autism generally cannot do this as objectively or as clearly. They are disabled by their inner feelings and are all too quick in interpreting and colouring behaviour.

The meaning behind behaviour, the sense or the impulses of conduct, is not easily grasped by people with autism. They are not good psychologists, and even less philosophers.[10] Because of their (hyper-) realism, people with autism have their feet more firmly on the ground than we. They miss out on the joys but also on the aggravations of our common illusions.

> She: I have had enough of this; I'm going back to my mother. Do you realise how much this is going to cost you?
>
> He: Forty pence for the bus ticket?

An artist with autism, Dan Esher, creates splendid video-art. He possesses an excellent eye for visual effects and can focus his attention on details that are overlooked by coherent thinkers. For instance, he will shoot a fountain where the water streams across a marble ball. The fountains reflects all of the surroundings: trees, houses, clouds. Dan Esher only zooms in on the water and so creates a magnificent image. Coherent thinkers take a while to realise that the water they see on the video images originates from a fountain because the surroundings, its context, have been left out.

Like Dan, there are other people with autism that have become famous for their ability in the graphic arts. Their drawings and paintings are generally very detailed and are technical gems. Very seldom, if ever, will you see in their art images of people – almost always just objects. Often, machines, trains and buildings are the principal subjects.

Kees Momma, a young man with autism from Holland, is one of those who can create exceptional drawings and models of churches. His work is finished to the smallest detail and the copies are perfect replicas of the real thing. Kees is a master in creating architectural detail with utmost precision. It was also a young boy with autism who created the drawings in the book you are reading now. It is striking – he was nine years old when he drew the pictures – how detailed his drawings of animals and plants were. As in the case of other talented individuals with autism, his drawings are little jewels when considered from an analytic point of view. But in general there is no real story behind the drawings. An autistic drawing is much more an image than imagination.

Their alternative thinking mode makes people with autism excel in areas where most coherent thinkers only grope around. In certain fields, people with autism perform much better than we do. They achieve better results with tasks that demand strict orientation, especially towards visual detail; with tasks where it is very important to work according to the rules, such as copying, classifying and certainly doing routine work. We are not that efficient in carrying out routine work since it is repetitive and we get bored quickly, and boredom leads to sloppiness.

Table 8.1: Strong points of people with and without autism	
Strong points of people with autism	**Strong points of people without autism**
Literal interpretation	Interpretation according to the spirit of things
Analytic thinking	Integrated thinking
Eye for detail	Eye for the whole picture
Serial processing of information	Parallel processing of information
Concrete things	Abstract things
Formal, logical rules	Non-logical things
Living according to the rules	Living between the lines
The facts	The ideas
The rules	Exceptions to the rules
Images	Imagination
Calculations	Intuitive feeling
Similarities	Analogies
Absolutes	Relatives
Objectivity	Subjectivity
Straightforward, honest	Elusive: humorous, deceptive
Perfectionism	Flexibility
The external	The internal
Deductive reasoning	Inductive reasoning
Realism	Surrealism
'This is the title'	'About autistic thinking'

Autism thus has its positive, strong points. And because autistic thinking is so different from normal thinking, it can in some cases lead to a special form of originality. It is not surprising, then, that people with autism are often inclined towards the artistic.

One of the features of autism, therefore, is its unequal development of the different forms of intelligence.[11] Those individuals with autism who do not have a learning disability are in no way less intelligent than other people; they happen to have a different kind of intelligence, another mode of thinking. People without autism tend to see the woods (the whole); individuals with autism focus on the trees (the parts). People with autism thus observe reality in a different light. That causes them a great deal of stress and disadvantage, but in some fields they realise achievements that are outstanding in comparison with their peers who do not have autism. (See Table 8.1)

Autistic thinking as survival strategy

Individuals with autism try to compensate for their shortcomings by accentuating their strong points, just as other people with disabilities do. Blind people, for instance, may compensate for their blindness by having a developed sense of hearing or smell. And deaf people are often extremely observant of the visual.

The same is true of people with autism. In order to survive, they make the best possible use of their strengths.

Witness Temple Grandin. In order to understand social situations and words better, she stores all kinds of video images inside her mind. Her strong capacity for the visual makes it possible for her to do so. She says she even thinks in pictures.[12] Images have helped her to learn the meaning of words: she collects, as it were, a picture of each word inside her head. When she hears a word, she calls up that picture and through it can see what the person means. Just like Temple, many other people with autism use their strongly developed sensitivity for the visual to survive.

People with autism also compensate using their excellent memory. Think back to our library without a classification system. In such a library you can only find your way around by remembering all the details. Equally, if you cannot associate events or meanings within their total context (a birthday party), you are thrown back on storing all details (yellow streamers, music, birthday cake with candles, presents, family, friends, Jan, Emma, and Chris). The outstanding memory in which some people with autism excel is not just a talent they happen to possess, for them it is compensation for their difficulties, a part of a necessary survival strategy.

Just like people with other kinds of disabilities, individuals with autism avoid situations that pose excessively difficult problems. Linda keeps on drinking Coke during a family party. She has already consumed a number of glasses and her father tells her she has had enough. Shortly afterwards, Linda grabs the Coke bottle from the table, opens the window, and pitches the bottle outside. By getting rid of the bottle she makes it disappear from her sight and she thus no longer needs to resist the urge to drink. As long as the Coke bottle is visible, the visual stimulus and thus the urge to drink is too strong for her. By pitching the bottle out of the window, she avoids that frustration.

It follows then that the action of compensating, by means of visual pictures, memory, avoidance behaviour etc., is dependent on the degree of general intelligence possessed by the individual with autism. Those with normal or advanced intelligence have more possibilities for compensation than those who are less well-endowed. It is, therefore, less easy to detect autism in the former group: in certain situations they come across as 'normal' and manage to hold their own, simply because they know how to compensate for their shortcomings.[13] Thus, the ability of those people with autism who have normal intelligence is often over-estimated.

One survival strategy that I have already described in various sections of this book is the calculation method. People with autism try to grasp situation through reason, calculation, classification – by resorting to and understanding logical and formal rules.

> Father and son are standing before the lion's cage at the zoo. The boy stands in thought for some time and then asks his father: 'Daddy, when the lion comes out of his cage and eats you, which bus must I take to get back home?'

> Leo, a young man who for years has had experiences with psychiatric wards and retains bad memories of them, tries to classify people and situations. His worst experiences with psychiatry dates from the time he stayed in Antwerp. Antwerp lies in the 03 telephone exchange, and so Leo used that detail as the basis of his classification system. All people and places from the 03 zone are 'bad', everyone and everything else is good (this sort of black-and-white sorting is typical of people with autism, e.g., mother = bad, father = good). When we want to go somewhere with Leo, he will always ask if the destination lies in the 03 zone. When Leo gets a new assistant in his course on social skills, he will ask if the newcomer lives in the 03 zone. New places, new people…they are unpredictable entities. On the basis of a formula (03 = bad), Leo tries to create some order and predictability in an unpredictable and incalculable world.

People without autism can live with open-ended situations. They take an attitude of 'we'll see'. They give new things a chance and, up to a certain point, can cope with life's unpredictability and fuzziness, falling back on their intuition. If you lack that intuition you need to create certainty in a different way. You need to draw up rules and categories, for instance, 03 = bad. That offers predict ability and thus the chance for survival.

We can get closer to people with autism when we do not simply romanticise their stronger skills into talents but consider them as functional survival strategies. When we want to help them, we have to build on that. Even so, many autistic actions (repetitive conduct, difficult behaviour) can be looked upon functionally as stress reactions: reactions to an environment that is proving too difficult and elusive to comprehend.

Common sense

In spite of all of the above-mentioned compensatory strategies, people with autism remain different. Complete autonomy and 'real' integration into the world of the coherent thinkers is possible for only a very small minority. Individuals with autism think differently and process information in a different way. To be different does not automatically mean that you are capable of less, but this does happen to be the case with autism. Autism is not just an alternative mode of thinking; it is a disability.

Many people with autism are disabled because they also have, aside from their autism, a learning disability. But even the normally intelligent people with autism have difficulties surviving in our society without assistance. The autistic way of thinking falls short when it comes to surviving within our world. Why?

People with autism (unless they are severely learning-disabled) assign meaning, or at least make major attempts at it, but their method of proceeding is different. It has no similarity to the usual way in which most people assign meanings. From that point of view, since individuals with autism do not give meaning in the way that non-autistics do, they do not possess 'common sence'.[14]

The term 'common sense' is a perfect indication of something 'communal'. Someone who lacks common sense is an outsider, he stands out, he falls outside the common societal scope. That is the case for people with autism. Because they assign meanings in an 'idiosyncratic' way (in contrast to 'communal'), they are singled out and cannot really participate in activities of groups at large. The kinds of meanings they assign are not shared by the great majority of people. That is their disability.

What does 'common sense' actually mean? And in what way do people with autism fall short in their use of common sense? What is the role of coherent thinking in common sense?

This is not easy to explain. The scientific understanding of how people know things, how they solve problems, how they think, remains limited even at the turn of the 20th century. But progress is being made, through inspiration derived from the world of computers; more specifically the world of artificial intelligence. If you want computers to carry out human assignments, you need first to find out how humans solve problems. And problems encountered in the development of intelligent machines tell us a lot about the human brain. With this subject, this book has come full circle and we are back to where we started.

'Up till now it has been impossibe to develop an artificial intelligent system that can use common sense',[15] wrote an authority in the field of artificial intelligence in the early 1990s. In spite of all spectacular attempts by computer programmers, we still do not have a computer with common sense. Whatever a computer's intelligence, it will never possess the common sense to decide to cross the street, even when confronted with a red 'stop' light.

Autism, like artificial intelligence, is not just a problem of knowledge or science. Parents of children with autism (especially when those children are of normal or high intelligence) know all about this. They regularly say: 'he knows it but he doesn't do it', or: 'he can explain as well as anyone how to behave in a store but when we get there, everything always goes awry…'.

This apparent absence of rhyme or reason (how can you know something and yet not do it?) is a major source of frustration and especially confusion for those of us confronted with autistic behaviour. It does, however, become a little less confusing, and thus more understandable, when we make a distinction between two kinds of knowledge: knowledge of facts and common sense (or 'know-how').[16]

Factual knowledge versus common sense

People with autism most frequently store factual knowledge. This kind of knowledge includes hard and well-defined data: definitions (a button man is a low-ranking member of an organised crime syndicate) and rules (when the light is red you must stop; when you see a uniform you must say 'hello'). Computers too are capable of storing this sort of knowledge. On the basis of factual knowledge you can identify things (aha, I know this man is not the big boss of the organisation but a low-ranking member, he is a button man) and control your conduct (I see a red light, so I stop).

A computer stores all these definitions and rules inside its memory, and nothing gets lost – just like the incredibly good memories of people with autism who remember details that have long-since been forgotten by others.

This knowledge of facts and rules seems sufficient, and so indeed it is for a large number of challenges and problems: mathematical problems, word translations, graphic making etc. But formulae are not enough for survival in the common world. As Astrid Nijgh, a Dutch singer, puts it: 'What good is algebra to me when I have to make choices?' Life is indeed more than definitions.

Two highway policemen sit in their car in front of a traffic light.

One says, 'It is green.'

'A frog,' replies his colleague.

An immediate problem with an extensive knowledge of facts is recalling them.[17] Computers assign every piece of information, every definition, every rule, a unique place in their memory. In computer terms, this is called 'an address'. Every address is given (like houses) a number. Each individual bit of information can only be retrieved via that one number, that unique address. As mentioned earlier on, a computer works using one-to-one relationships. One bit of information = one address. The computer cannot get data from its memory if the number of the address where the information is stored is not entered.

> 'Artificial intelligence programs do not possess common sense, little feel for agreement, repetition, or pattern. They can observe certain patterns in cases where they have been prepared for them – and identify them by name provided they have been prepared for the place where the patterns are located – but they are incapable of seeing patterns when there is no explicit command to look them up.'[18]

You will often hear people with autism make the same statement: they do not know what to do until somebody has 'pressed' the right key, given the right instruction. They are dependent on the instruction that tells them where to find the rule that needs to be applied in a given situation. They just cross the street until somebody directs them to take a look at the colour of the traffic light. They know what to do but they don't do it.

When you are not dependent on concrete facts and rules but can detect cohesion and apply it to the world around you, your memory functions in a different way. It is not necessary for every fact in life to be assigned a fixed and unique address in our memory in order to be recalled again. We do not need 'numbers' to remember things. Our memory is organised according to an open system whereby information is usually retrieved on the basis of multiple (not just one) descriptions. Imagine that, last night, you were at Richard's place and the two of you watched a football game on TV. After that you had some pizza. In order for you to remember what you had to eat it is not necessary to ask one very specific, question. The pizza forms part of a much broader whole of descriptive parts (yesterday, at Richard's place, football match) and every single one of these descriptions will allow us to call up the pizza from our memory. It doesn't much matter what sort of question is asked ('What did you eat last night?' or 'What did you have to eat when you were at Richard's place watching football on TV?').

The ultimate cohesion is of course the one of your own personal life. Since individuals with autism detect much less cohesion, they are dependent on their memory of details. And if the correct address is not given, nothing much will happen, even though the answers are contained in the memory.

Therein lies the fundamental limitation in developing learning programmes for students with autism. You can teach them an array of definitions (corners of the mouth downwards and tears = sadness) and rules (if you want to speak up in class you need to raise your hand), but first the right key needs to be pressed, the correct hint given, before the proper and expected reaction will occur. What they learn is imbedded in a broad collection of descriptions wherein they can delve and dig and make flexible choices to a much lesser degree.[19]

Autism is more than a memory problem – it is much more than a problem of saving, storing, and retrieving knowledge. To participate fully in the world of people, knowledge of facts and logic do not suffice. You also need a good portion of common sense. Common sense, the most human form of intelligence, does not operate according to the rules of logic: it is 'chaotic' and 'slippery'.[20] It is the art of guessing correctly.[21] In this case 'guessing' means being flexible in dealing with ideas and notions. This sort of flexibility is irreconcilable with the strict rules of logic. Coherent thinkers do not need rules and definitions, they are able to assess things in the blink of an eye: 'Aha, that's how it works…'. They recognise patterns and situations without knowing in advance what to look for, through making an instant assessment of the situation. This does not happen on the basis of knowledge of facts but on the basis of 'know-how' and 'feeling'. It does not require conscious thought but rather intuition.[22] For that reason, common sense cannot be taught or programmed.

Babies possess this know-how. A baby sees and feels the teat. She 'knows' it is there for sucking on. She feels it instinctively, intuitively. No need to go looking first for a rule or a definition. Obviously, this is an instinct also possessed by animals. Gradually, the same baby will in other circumstances, in complex social situations, make evaluations based on instincts like this. The know-how will keep on increasing.

As people with autism grow up, their knowledge of facts (the knowledge of rules and definitions) grows as well, sometimes in leaps and bounds; but their know-how remains lower than other people's. This happens because knowledge of facts and know-how evolve along different lines. If knowledge of facts increases, it is because new 'data' and new facts are being added. Know-how increases not only through the addition of new data but also because existing knowledge is developed so that it can be used in novel situations. Although no new knowledge is being added, existing knowledge may be broadened. This broadening happens in the human brain on the basis of analogies. This is where human intelligence differs from that of computers. Humans are capable of detecting analogies and thus of manipulating ideas in a flexible manner. Analogies are things or situations that may look different on the surface but are strongly similar in their essence.[23]

Computers and people with autism have difficulties with analogies. They generalise on the basis of similarities. Think back to previous sections in this book about over-generalisation and hyper-selectivity. That computer and individuals with autism act literally is due to a different organisation of their knowledge, which is classified on the basis of identical comparisons, exact agreements and details.

Computers and individuals with autism need lengthy and detailed descriptions for ideas. It is necessary to describe all possible elements in our red traffic light situation. When the light is red and you haven't started to cross yet, stay where you are. When the light turns red and you are halfway across the road, keep on going. When… And so on and so on. When there occurs a situation that is identical to one of the situations that have been entered or learned, there is no problem.

Alas, life doesn't have all that many identical situations. Usually, we get ourselves into situations that 'resemble' one another. We move from one station to the next and none is identical to the other, even though they are all stations along the same route. They are quasi-alike but not entirely alike. They are similar, meaning that they belong to the same category, even though they may differ externally on the detail level. We recognise this similarity because we know how to handle 'analogies'.

One example will suffice: when I say that the Rolls Royce is the king of the motor cars, you know immediately what I mean. But for the person who thinks in literal terms, in terms of the logic of rules, definitions, and facts, what I'm saying is absurd, ridiculous and illogical. Surely a car can never be king. There is no (exact) association between a king and a car. People who need exact definitions, like the computer, get terribly confused by this sort of pronouncement. However, to be attuned to this sort of vague association is the hallmark of human and flexible intelligence.[24]

Human know-how deals with vague associations and analogies all the time. These are completely different from the literal, formal criteria of logic, which uses exact similarities, definitions and rules: they are only 'absurdity yardsticks'.[25]

One mother wrote an article for the Flemish magazine *Autisme* wherein she placed the ever-progressive distinction of sub-groups within the autistic spectrum in perspective.[26] She wrote that one can so over-emphasise the differences between children with autism that ultimately every sub-group would be left with just one child. And as her own son was named Thomas, she called this 'the Thomas syndrome' by way of example and analogy.

Some time thereafter I received a letter from a young lady with autism, Elisabeth, who was herself struggling with her diagnosis. She asked for information about the 'kinds of autism', including

Asperger syndrome. She ended her letter by asking: '...and could you perhaps give me some details about the Thomas syndrome?'

Between the lines

People with autism like clear rules and definitions, because they function better in a world governed by clarity and unambiguity. A world where cars can become kings – no, that's too surreal for them. Individuals with autism are capable of learning many facts, rules and definitions. And as long as the situations in which they find themselves caught up, the problems that confront them, are literally identical to the rules and definitions they know of, they feel they can manage. If all toilet seats were identical (white), there would be no problem for Mark.

Unfortunately, the world is not to be taken literally, in terms of black-white relationships. Our world is one of open-ended 'almost situations'.[27] No everyday situation can be categorised just by rules or definitions. A uniform does not always require a greeting.

No situation is literally identical to another but many are analogous to each other. Leslie one day wears a green sweater, the next a red one. In spite of the difference in sweaters, she is expected to raise her hand before speaking.

The similarities, the analogies, do not confine themselves to the level of details but always to the level of the abstract, to the cohesion between things (the Rolls Royce stands in relation to other cars the way a king stands in relation to his subjects).

Many situations do not admit of unambiguous rules and in so far as rules exist, they are changeable and invisible. Potatoes now are cut into chunks, now in strips. Real life cannot be compartmentalised in rigid interpretations of rules and definitions.

People with autism have a disability because life does not unfold along regulated lines. They experience problems with the vagueness of it all: real life is played out in-between the lines.

Life does not so much demand an encyclopaedic knowledge of facts, an area where computers and people with autism excel, as it does an intuitive know-how. That is why computers cannot change nappies. Knowing traffic rules, the map of Belgium or the brands of the different lamps used for lighting roads and highways will not help you drive a car. Driving a car requires much more than geographic knowledge, ability to read technical data or obedience to rules. It requires feeling and know-how, a feeling for distance and speed, correct anticipation of other drivers on the road, ability to manoeuvre your way confidently in traffic. Driving a car is like dancing along the road (and notice here we have yet another analogy!).

Computers and people with autism will always remain challenged in their carrying out of everyday activities. Driving a car, making coffee, talking with the mailman, all these activities presuppose so much trivial and banal knowledge that is just not 'learnable'. (Bananas don't grow on dogs, pitchers always fall downwards and shatter into pieces, in the winter you wear warm clothes, you can get badly burned by boiling water, cows don't smoke cigars…).

A student in gynaecology assisted in a birth as part of his Finals.

After the birth, the examining professor said to him: 'Johnson, that was first class. You did everything according to the book. I have just one observation: it is the newborn baby's bottom you have to slap, not the mother's.'

You cannot calculate human behaviour. Anger cannot be expressed on a scale from 1 to 100 (see the example earlier in the book). Many situations can only be understood intuitively on the basis of analogies because no one situation is identical to another in every detail.

We can teach people with autism a lot of knowledge and behavioural rules, but this is merely a bandage on the wound. Autism, the other way of thinking, the non-intuitive mode of thinking, the absence of intuitive comprehension of the cohesion between things…will always be present to exert its influence.

Carl, a man with autism, loved to play squash. When he came down from the dressing room on his way to the courts, he would call out to the barman: 'Which court?' His assistant told him this was not polite. He should ask this sort of question at the bar, not shout it out from afar. Next time, Carl went to the bar counter and asked his question. Except...at the time, there was nobody at the bar.

A disability is never without some social significance. It is more than just the disorder. It is a disorder in a social setting. By themselves, motor disorders are not necessarily disabilities. They only turn into disabilities in a society that presupposes mobility.

The different mode of thinking, typical of individuals with autism, is a clear disability when you consider that our present society demands enormous wisdom, common sense, flexibility and ability to generalise. There have always been people with autism but only now are they really missing the boat. In the past, when society was much less complex and obsessed with time, when there were far more rules – dictated and not subject to discussion – when the whole of our social structure was much more simple (a clearly defined hierarchy where everybody had his expected place) – in those times people with autism could still survive. Granted, they were a bit strange, but they were surviving.

For certain types of jobs, people with autism were ideally suited, better than anybody else. Who, indeed, is better at classifying than a person with autism? For this sort of job you need an eye for detail and you need to apply the rules. No flexibility is required. Imagine if you were to start classifying according to the way you feel as you go along! For a large number of jobs, the precision and logic of the autistic computer-type thinking is an asset. The disadvantage today is that this sort of job has been taken over by computers, which do it better and faster, so that individuals with autism are no longer in great demand in the labour market. Modern society no

longer needs people who excel in classifying or counting or calculating.

Fast and analytic thinking, efficiency and flexibility are rated a
lot higher in our society. Look at the vacancy ads in the papers –
they are for jobs that computers cannot undertake. Counsellors,
housekeepers, barmen, are needed these days, but they are the
kinds of jobs for which people with autism are not well-suited. The
fact that our society has become more complex and operates on
fewer fixed rules provides increased challenges to people with
autism.

Yet, all of this has to be placed in its proper perspective. Sometimes, intuition falls short. In such cases, the ability to think in
details and adhere to formal rules and definitions becomes an ad-
vantage. Imagine for a moment that bridges and aeroplanes were
built on intuition only instead of by exact calculations; that physi-
cians prescribed drugs only on the basis of individual judgement,
without adjusting their dosage to relevant factors such as, for
example, the weight, height and age of a child patient.

> 'Be aware! Do not assume that literal interpretation and applica-
> tion is to be avoided at all cost. If the preference were always
> towards the adaptation of levels of abstraction, we would ulti-
> mately wind up not making any distinctions between situations
> at all. The optimal description of each and every situation would
> be: 'something is happening'.[28]

With this pronouncement an expert in the field of artificial intelligence situated the superiority of human intelligence in relation to
the intelligence of the computer. He continued as follows: 'There
are many forms of rigidity and a rigid inclination towards abstrac-
tion is as dumb as a rigid refusal to engage in the act of abstracting.'

People with autism are in fact no less intelligent than people
without autism. They just possess another kind of intelligence that
makes them process stimuli in a different way. This makes them a
'challenged' group. Their reliance on the 'literal', their eye for

detail, their following of strict, formal rules and definitions and their concrete way of thinking no longer satisfies the demands of modern society. Because of this they have become outsiders, archaic and estranged Sherlock Holmes characters, or robots *before letters*. Their mode of thinking is considered eccentric. Yet in their eccentricity a separate sort of creativity lies hidden, a creativity that not infrequently passes by the ordinary, common, flexible, discerning and abstract-thinking person of our modern times.

It is a challenge for all coherent thinkers to assign a place in our society for people who think in literal terms. But people with autism have need of more than just help. They deserve appreciation for being themselves. They can, if we allow them to do so, contribute in a meaningful way to our society. We do not need to offer individuals with autism a place in our society *in spite* of their autism, we need to offer them a place *because* of their autism. Our society can profit from a little more of autism. As Francesca Happé suggests,[29] the weak central coherence of people with autism should not be considered just as a deficit; it is better characterised in terms of a cognitive style. Their strong points (see Table 8.1 above) are often our own weak points. Being oriented towards the literal does not just mean a predisposition to naïvety: sometimes a literal interpretation brings us back to reality.

'Why are you spending all day in front of your computer?'

'I'm writing a book about autistic thinking.'

'But why? You can buy that stuff for £10.'

In conclusion: this book is primarily meant for coherent thinkers, for those who can grasp an idea on the basis of analogies, who can handle yardsticks that define the absurd. When I compare the thinking of people with autism with the data processing of computers, I realise that that too is an analogy, not an identification. People who think in literal terms will wrongly compare the similarity of things to the identical; so to compare people with autism with computers is ostensibly absurd and deserves our ridicule. In the way that the idea that a Rolls Royce could ever be a king is laughable.

This is a little book for those who have the ability to read intuitively, not according to the formal rules of logic. The message isn't expressed in the lines but between the lines.

Notes

1.   Vroon (1992, p.233).

2.   Van Dalen (1995a, p.14).

3.   See also Vroon (1992). The term 'central control unity' (CCU) derives from Gazzaniga (1985). This CCU has no identifiable location in the brain, although there are indications that the left cerebral cortex plays a role in the creation of that central decision-making and processing system. CCU is thus a hypothetical construct, a mechanism, rather than a defined location in the brain as such. It is known that the function of the CCU in people with autism usually occurs in the *right* half of the brain: holistic instead of logical-analytic.

      Theories formed around the CCU point to a possible neurological foundation of the central coherence problem in autism. Vroon states: 'Many researchers believe (in consequence) that people with autism have a badly developed CCU' (1992, p.223).

      Vroon's observation regarding the fact that children with autism do not properly focus their attention (see quote at the beginning of this chapter) finds support in the many studies by Eric Courchesne concerning the problems with 'attention shifting'. This problem with attention focusing is an important early warning signal for autism. According to Courchesne (1996), the cerebellum is responsible for the selection of incoming stimuli and is the co-ordinator of other brain zones.

4.   Though there still appear new theories and therapies that hold to the notion that people with autism are kinds of intellectual prisoners of their disability. This notion, for instance, lies at the basis of 'Facilitated Communication', a method which assumes that persons with autism are very sensitive and intelligent individuals who, however, cannot communicate unless they receive 'a helping or guiding hand'.

5.   Weizenbaum (1977). The quote is taken from the Dutch translation, 1984, p.224.

6.   See Vermeulen (1995a, 1995b, 1996).

7.   There are, however, computers – the latest generation of artificial intelligence machines (the so-called neural networks of PDP computers: Parallel Distributed Processing) – that can process information in a parallel way. What is remarkable about these computers is that they, in contrast to the serially processing computers, can work with context (Copeland 1993).

8.   See Van Dalen (1995b).

9.   Hermelin and O'Connor (1970) did not supply this drawing but rather drawings from a test called the 'Embedded Figures Test'.

10.   For further reading on this deficit in 'folk psychology' see Baron-Cohen (2000).

11. Integrating intelligence plays such an important role in the development and learning process that the growth of other areas of knowledge and skills depends on it. For that reason, people with autism lag behind their peer group in a number of developmental areas. With justice, one may refer to a 'pervasive' or intrusive 'developmental disorder'.

12. Temple Grandin (1996).

13. It has been demonstrated that quite a number of older and more intelligent people with autism succeed in tests that people with autism normally fail, such as the Sally-Ann experiment relating to theory of mind. Further studies of these surprising results revealed that some of these people arrived at the correct answer via a different strategy to that adopted by people without autism.

14. See Frith (1989). Uta Frith is not the first to offer this idea. Hans Asperger (1944) already formulated the notion that autistic intelligence possessed distinct qualities and could be described as the opposite of worldly wisdom.

15. Marvin L. Minsky (1992, pp.356–358).

16. Frith (1989, p.89) refers to the difference between 'test intelligence' and 'world intelligence'.
    For the two kinds of knowledge that I have described here, some neurological evidence is available. The left part of the brain is the storehouse of logic, of sequential reasoning; the right side is more 'holistic': the part of the brain that is the seat of wisdom and of one's intuition, the half that works with metaphors and analogies (see Weizenbaum 1984, p.234).

17. For more details see Chapter 9 of Copeland (1993).

18. Hofstadter (1985). The quote is taken from the Dutch translation of 1988, p.639.

19. Herein lies the explanation of the so-called 'person dependency' or instruction dependency of people with autism.

20. The terms 'chaotic' and 'slippery' are from Vroon (1992, p.196).

21. H.B. Barlow, *The Oxford Companion to the Mind*, in A. Penzias (1990). (The quote is taken form the Dutch translation of Penzias, p.114.)

22. Courchesne (1996) situates this intuition in the cerebellum. The cerebellum prepares us *subconsciously* for what is about to happen. Damage to the cerebellum leads to incorrect or delayed reactions and makes it necessary to think consciously prior to reacting.
    According to Hofstadter (1985), common sense has to do with 'sub-cognition'. Computers can execute cognitive activities but lack the sub-cognition that forms the basis of common sense and human flexibility.

23. As mentioned earlier in the section on problem solving, there is a strong suspicion that people with autism are better at deductive than at inductive reasoning. Inductive reasoning uses the identification of analogies.

24. Hofstadter (1985). The quote is taken from the Dutch translation, 1988, p.559.

25. Weizenbaum (1977). The quote is taken from the Dutch translation, 1984, p.236.

26. De Clercq (1993).

27. Jordan and Powell (1995, p.31).

28. Hofstadter (1985). The quote taken from the Dutch translation, 1988, p.584.

29. Happé (1999).

Bibliography
About reference works consulted

Asperger, H. (1944) 'Die "Autistischen Psychopathen" im Kindesalter.' *Archiv für Psychiatrie und Nervenkrankheiten 117*, 76–136.

Asperger, H. (1991) 'Autistic psychopathy in childhood.' In U. Frith (ed.), *Autism and Asperger Syndrome* (pp. 37–92). Cambridge/New York: Cambridge University Press. (Translated and annotated by U. Frith.)

Bailey, A. *et al.* (1996) 'Autism: Towards an integration of clinical, genetic, neuropsychological and neurobiological perspectives.' *Journal of Child Psychology and Psychiatry 37*, 1, 89–126.

Baron-Cohen, S. (1995) *Mindblindness: An Essay on Autism and Theory of Mind.* London: The MIT Press.

Baron-Cohen, S. (2000) 'Autism: Deficits in folk psychology exist alongside superiority in folk physics.' In S. Baron-Cohen, H. Tager-Flusberg and D. J. Cohen (eds) *Understanding Other Minds: Perspectives from Developmental Cognitive Neuroscience, Second Edition.* Oxford/New York: Oxford University Press.

Baron-Cohen, S., Tager-Flusberg, H. and Cohen, D.J. (eds) (2000) *Understanding Other Minds: Perspectives From Developmental Cognitive Neuroscience, Second Edition.* Oxford/New York: Oxford University Press.

Berckelaer-Onnes, I.A. van (1992) *Leven naar de Letter* ('Living by the Book'). Groningen: Wolters-Noordhoff. (Living by the book)

Bergsma, A. (1994) 'Grappen als mentale vakantie.' *Tijdschrift voor Psychologie 13*, April, 16–18.

Blundell, N. (1983) *Het Grote Blunderboek.* Baarn: In den Toren. (English translation, 1983, *The World's Greatest Mistakes.* London: Octopus Books.)

Copeland, J. (1993) *Artificial Intelligence: A Philosophical Introduction.* Oxford: Blackwell.

Courchesne, E. (1996) 'Abnormal cerebellar activity in autism alters cortical and subcortical systems.' Lecture held at the Fifth European Congress on Autism in Barcelona on 3 May, 1996.

De Clercq, H. (1993) 'Zwanger? Neen, enkel in verwachting.' ('Pregnant? No, only expectant.) *Autisme 12*, 4, 24–31.

Frith, U. (1989) *Autism: Explaining the Enigma.* Oxford and New York: Basil Blackwell.

Gaarder, J. (1994) *De Wereld van Sofie: roman over de Geschiedenis van de Filosofie.* Antwerpen: Houtekiet/Fontein. (Translated into English in 1995 as *Sophie's World: An Adventure in Philosophy.* London: Phoenix House.)

Gazzaniga, M.S. (1985) *The Social Brain.* New York: Basic Books.

Gerland, G. (1996) *En Riktig Människa.* Stockholm: Cura. (Translated into English in 1997 as *A Real Person: Life on the Outside.* London: Souvenir Press.)

Gillberg, C. (1990) 'Artistic talents in autism.' Lecture held in Antwerp (Belgium) on 6 October, 1990.

Grandin, T. (1992) 'An inside view of autism.' In E. Schopler and G.B. Mesibov (eds) *High-Functioning Individuals with Autism.* New York/London: Plenum Press.

Grandin, T. (1995) *Thinking in Pictures.* New York: Doubleday.

Grandin, T. (1995) 'How people with autism think.' In E. Schopler and G.B. Mesibov (eds) *Learning and Cognition in Autism.* New York/London: Plenum Press.

Gray, C. A. (1998) 'Social stories and comic strip conversations with students with Asperger syndrome and high-functioning autism.' In E. Schopler, G. B. Mesibov and L. J. Kunce (eds), *Asperger Syndrome or High-Functioning Autism?* (pp. 167–198). New York/London: Plenum Press.

Happé, F. (1994) *Autism: An Introduction to Psychological Theory.* London: UCL Press.

Happé, F. (1999) 'Autism: Cognitive deficit or cognitive style?' Paper presented at the Autism99 internet conference: www.autism99.org/ Nov. 1999.

Happé, F. (2000) 'Parts and wholes, meaning and minds: Central coherence and its relation to theory of mind.' In S. Baron-Cohen, H. Tager-Flusberg and D. J. Cohen (eds) *Understanding Other Minds: Perspectives from Developmental Cognitive Neuroscience, Second edition.* Oxford/New York: Oxford University Press.

Hart, C. (1989) *Without Reason.* Harmondsworth/New York: Penguin Books.

Hay, D.F., Stimson, C. and Castle, J. (1991) 'A meeting of minds in infancy: Imitation and desire.' In D. Frye and C. Moore (eds) *Children's Theories of Minds: Mental States and Social Understanding.* Hillsdale, N.J.: Lawrence Erlbaum.

Hermelin, B. and O'Connor, N. (1970) *Psychological Experiments with Autistic Children.* London: Pergamon Press.

Hofstadter, D.R. (1979) *Gödel, Escher and Bach: An Eternal Golden Braid.* New York: Basic Books.

Hofstadter, D.R. (1985) *Metamagical Themas: Questing for the Essence of Mind and Pattern.* New York: Basic Books.

Hughes, C., Russell, J. and Robbins, T. (1994) 'Specific planning deficit in autism: Evidence of a central executive dysfunction.' *Neuropsychologic 3,* 474–492.

Jolliffe, T., Lansdown, R. and Robinson, C. (1992) 'Autism: A personal account.' *Communication 26,* 3, 12–19.

Jordan, R. and Powell, S. (1995) *Understanding and Teaching Children with Autism.* Chichester/New York: John Wiley and Sons.

Kanner, L. (1943) 'Autistic disturbances of affective contact.' *Nervous Child 2,* 217–250.

Kosinski, J. (1971) *Being There.* New York: Bantam Books.

Leekam, S. (1996) 'Features of autism in normally developing children.' Lecture held at the Fifth European Congress on Autism in Barcelona on 3 May 1996.

Minsky, M. L. (1992) 'Future of AI technology.' *Toshiba Review 47*, 356–358.

Momma, K. (1996) *En toen Verscheen een Regenboog. Hoe ik mijn Autistische Leven Ervaar. ('And then a Rainbow Appeared: How I Experience my Autistic Life.')* Amsterdam: Prometheus.

Mulders, M.A.H., Hansen, M.A.T. and Roosen, C.J.A. (1996) *Autisme: Aanpassen en Veranderen: Handboek voor Ambulante Praktijk. ('Autism: Adapting and Changing: Handbook for Non-Residential Practice')* Assen: Van Gorcum.

Newson, E. (2000) 'Using humour to enable flexibility and social empathy in children with Asperger's syndrome: some practical strategies.' In S. Powell (ed) *Helping Children with Autism to Learn* (pp. 94–106). London: David Fulton Publishers.

Ozonoff, S. (1995) 'Executive functions in autism.' In: E. Schopler and G.B. Mesibov (eds) *Learning and Cognition in Autism*. New York/London: Plenum Press.

Paulos, J.A. (1985) *I Think, Therefore I Laugh: An Alternative Approach to Philosophy*. New York: Columbia University Press.

Peeters, T. (1997) *Autism: From Theoretical Understanding to Educational Intervention*. London: Whurr.

Peeters, T. and Gillberg, C. (1998) *Autism: Medical and Educational Aspects*. London: Whurr.

Penzias, A. (1990) *Information and Technology: Managing in a High-Tech World*. New York: W.W. Norton.

Phillips, W., Gómez, J. C., Baron-Cohen, S., Laá, V. and Rivière, A. (1995) 'Treating people as objects, agents, or "subjects": How young children with and without autism make requests.' *Journal of Child Psychology and Psychiatry 36*, 8, 1383–1398.

Quill, K. (ed) (1995) *Teaching Children with Autism: Strategies to Enhance Communication and Socialization*. New York/London: Delmar Publishers.

Sacks, O. (1995) *An Anthropologist on Mars*. London: Picador.

Sinclair, J. (1992) 'Bridging the gaps: An inside-out view of autism.' In E. Schopler and G. B. Mesibov (eds) *High-Functioning Individuals with Autism* (pp. 294–302). New York/London: Plenum Press.

Szatmari, P. (1998) 'Differential diagnosis of Asperger disorder.' In E. Schopler, G.B. Mesibov and L.J. Kunce (eds) *Asperger Syndrome or High-Functioning Autism?* New York/London: Plenum Press.

Twachtman, D.D. (1995) 'Methods to enhance communication in verbal children.' In K. Quill (ed) (1995) *Teaching Children with Autism: Strategies to Enhance Communication and Socialization*. New York/London: Delmar Publishers.

Van Bourgondiën, M. E. and Mesibov, G. B. (1987) 'Humor in high-functioning autistic adults.' *Journal of Autism and Developmental Disorders 17*, 3, 417–424.

Van Dalen, J.G.T. (1995a) 'Autism from within: looking through the eyes of a mildly afflicted autistic person.' *Link 17*, 11–16.

Van Dalen, J.G.T. (1995b) 'Autisme: Weinig keus?' ('Autism: Not much choice?') *Engagement 22*, 4, 7–11.

Vermeulen, P. (1994) 'Autisme en het gezin. Een verhaal van perplexiteit.' ('Autism and the family: A story about perplexity') *Tijdschrift voor Welzijnswerk 18*, 182, 81–89.

Vermeulen, P. (1995a) 'Wat is intelligentie? Autisme en intelligentie, deel 1.' ('Autism and intelligence.') *Autisme 14*, 5, 10–14. (The journal of the Vlaamse Dienst Autisme.)

Vermeulen, P. (1995b) 'Wat is een I.Q.? Autism en intelligentie, deel 2.' *Autisme 14*, 6, 31–33.

Vermeulen, P. (1996) 'Als we hen intensief stimuleren? Autisme en intelligente, deel 3.' *Autisme 15*, 5, 24–32.

Vermeulen, P. (1997) *Een Gesloten Boek: Autisme en Emoties* ('A closed book: Autism and emotions'). Ghent: Vlaamse Dienst Autisme.

Vermeulen, P. (1998) 'Some impressions on autism and art: Being au/rtistic.' *Link 24*, 3, 10–11.

Vermeulen, P. (1999) *Brein Bedriegt: Als Autisme niet Op Autisme Lijkt* ('Brain Cheats: When Autism doesn't Look Like Autism'). Berchem/Ghent: EPO/Vlaamse Dienst Autisme.

Vlaamse Vereniging Autisme (1987) 'Autisme: Voorbereiden op volwassenheid.' ('Autism: Preparing for adulthood.') Conference held on 16 May 1987 at the Vlaamse Vereniging Autism, Ghent.

Vroon, P. (1992) *Wolfsklem: De Evolutie van het Menselijk Gedrag* ('Wolf's trap: The evolution of human behaviour'). Baarn: Ambo.

Wechsler, D. (1992) *Manual for the Wechsler Intelligence Scale for Children – Revised.* Antonio, TX: Psychological Corporation.

Weizenbaum, J. (1977) *Computer Power and Human Reason: From Judgment to Calculation.* New York: Freeman.

Weizenbaum, J. (1984) *Computerkracht en Mensenkracht: Van Oordeel tot Berekening.* Amsterdam: Contact.

Index